CONTENTS

1) Introduction to John Donne — 1
2) The Anniversary Poems — 6
3) Songs and Sonnets — 19
4) Elegies — 51
5) Epicedes and Obsequies — 54
6) Satyres — 57
7) Verse Letters — 60
8) Divine Poems — 63
9) Introduction to George Herbert — 72
10) The Collar — 73
11) The Pulley — 75
12) The Altar — 77

13)	Easter-Wings	79
14)	Jordan	80
15)	Introduction to Abraham Cowley	81
16)	To the Royal Society	82
17)	Ode: Of Wit	85
18)	The Wish	87
19)	Introduction to Henry Vaughan	89
20)	The World	90
21)	The Retreat	92
22)	Critical Commentary	94
23)	Essay Questions and Answers	101
24)	Bibliography	106
25)	Subject Bibliography and Guide to Research Papers	110
26)	Suggested Research Papers	112

BRIGHT NOTES

THE METAPHYSICAL POETS

Intelligent Education

Nashville, Tennessee

BRIGHT NOTES: The Metaphysical Poets
www.BrightNotes.com

No part of this publication may be used or reproduced in any manner whatsoever without written permission, except in the case of brief quotations in critical articles and reviews. For permissions, contact Influence Publishers http://www.influencepublishers.com.

ISBN: 978-1-645424-62-8 (Paperback)
ISBN: 978-1-645424-63-5 (eBook)

Published in accordance with the U.S. Copyright Office Orphan Works and Mass Digitization report of the register of copyrights, June 2015.

Originally published by Monarch Press.
1982
2020 Edition published by Influence Publishers.

Interior design by Lapiz Digital Services. Cover Design by Thinkpen Designs.

Printed in the United States of America.

Library of Congress Cataloging-in-Publication Data forthcoming.
Names: Intelligent Education
Title: BRIGHT NOTES: The Metaphysical Poets
Subject: STU004000 STUDY AIDS / Book Notes

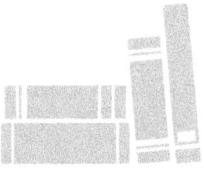

JOHN DONNE

INTRODUCTION

EARLY LIFE

John Donne was born in 1572, of well-to-do Roman Catholic parents. His early training was received under the Jesuits, from whom he undoubtedly learned much of the subtle scholastic logic which enhances (or infects) his poetry, but from who he must also have received instruction in the devotional attitudes which inform so much of his religious verse. He had roots going deep into medieval Catholicism. (His brother died in Newgate prison, where he had been confined for harboring a priest.) For some time after 1584 Donne attended the universities of Oxford and Cambridge, but was debarred, as a Catholic, from taking a degree. In his early twenties (the 1590s) he took part in London social life, while reading law at the Inns of Court, and it is from this period that most of his love lyrics, as well as the **satires** and elegies must date. He was beset by religious doubts and was probably reading deeply in theological literature, in the effort to settle upon some religious persuasion.

BEGINNING CAREER AND MARRIAGE

In 1596 - 97 he was a member of the Spanish expedition led by Essex, and, upon his return in 1598, received an appointment as secretary to Sir Thomas Egerton. During this time he fell in love with Ann More, the niece of Sir Thomas Egerton's second wife, and they were secretly married in 1601. (Walton, in his *Life of Dr. John Donne*, calls it "the remarkable error of his life.") Ann's irate father, Sir George More, succeeded in having Donne dismissed and cast into prison. By 1609 he had been reconciled to Donne, at least to the extent of paying a dowry, but the intervening years must have been a continual search for a patron. In 1611 Donne published his *An Anatomie of the World (The First Anniversary)*, an extravagant **elegy** on the death of a young girl unknown to him, but a poem with profound philosophical ramifications. She was Elizabeth Drury, the daughter of Sir Robert Drury, who, as a result of the hyperbolical praise lavished on his daughter, became Donne's benefactor and patron, providing him with a house, which Donne with his fast-growing family was sorely in need of. In 1612 there followed *The Progresse of the Soule (The Second Anniversary)*, an equally extravagant and obscure poem in memory of Elizabeth Drury.

FURTHUR WRITINGS AND LATER LIFE

At this time he was also giving expression to serious reflections in prose, writing *Biathanatos* (1608), an analysis of the morality of suicide, *Essayes in Divinity* (1614), *Pseudo-Martyr* (1610), a defense of the opinion that Catholics should take the Oath of Allegiance, and *Ignatius His Conclave* (1611), a **satire** built around the rival claims of various "new thinkers" to Ignatius' throne in Hell; only the last two were published, the former two being printed after Donne's death. When it became clear that preferments would be open to him only if he entered Holy Orders, Donne was ordained in the Anglican church in 1615. For some years after 1616 he preached at Lincoln's Inn, where, in the 1590s he had studied and made many friends. The great tragedy and permanent sorrow of his life was the death of his wife in 1617. Ann More, through all the poverty and uncertainty they had faced together, had borne him twelve children, seven of whom survived. In 1621 Donne was made Dean of St. Paul's, in which post he composed and preached many of the voluminous sermons he left behind. A serious illness in 1623 produced his *Devotions Upon Emergent Occasions* (containing, among others, the famous "No man is an island" and "Ask not for whom the bell tolls" passages). In 1631 he rose from his sickbed and preached the famous sermon known as Death's Duel before the King. He died shortly thereafter.

BRIEF SUMMARY OF THE POETRY OF DONNE

Songs And Sonnets

These are the poems most often read and studied. Probably written mainly in the 1590s, they display a variety of attitudes ranging from cynical wit, through impudent jocularity, to genuine passion. They are difficult, "witty" performances, for the most part, showing the effect of Donne's wide reading and scholastic training. Though some of the lyrics are songs (and, if fact, a number were set to music) the majority are marked by irregular and difficult rhythms and grammatical complication, which, together with their devil-may-care tone, have given Donne a reputation as a very "masculine" sort of poet. (It is significant that what we call "**metaphysical**" wit was referred to in the seventeenth century as "strong lines.") He challenges stale, conventional poses, such as the literary posturing of Courtly

Love poets, applies ingenious scholastic subtleties (such as the difference between essence and existence) to the analysis of the emotions of lovers, insists upon seeing present human joys and delights in the light of the dissolution which awaits us in the grave, and generally flies in the face of the pretty, sanctified notions about men and women in love which had permeated the love poetry of the preceding decades.

In these poems we are confronted by the immemorial war between the body and the soul, strained through a subtle intelligence and a sensitive spirit. The "**metaphysical**" style, as we encounter it in these poems, seems the natural vehicle for expressing a sense of the tensions between matter and spirit, faith and reason, between comfortable Aristotelian cosmology and disturbing "new philosophy." If, as Johnson remarked, the **metaphysical** poets "yoked their images together by violence," that violence was an inheritance from a century of theological, philosophical, and political wrangling, and would continue through the Jacobean period to culminate in a bloody civil war.

Other Short Poems

The *Elegies*, which witty, gay (and in some instances, frankly sensual) performances in the style of Ovid, and deal with such subjects as the betrayal to his mistress' father of a secret lover by the scent from the perfume he wore, probably belong to the carefree early days. So too with the *Satyres*, which deal with fops, venal lawyers, religious sectaries, fawning courtiers, and a number of other "humorous" types to be found in the London of the 1590s. The *Verse Letters* are difficult to date and assign; they are frequently merely exaggerated compliments, showing Donne in the guise of one who had to seek out and maintain favorable alliances, but their range proves him to have had a wide group of acquaintances among the court circle.

Elegies

Donne composed a number of "epicedes and obsequies" on the occasion of the deaths of famous persons (like that on Prince Henry) or those connected with the families of his patrons (such as the poem on the death of Lord Harrington, brother of the Countess of Bedford). The most impressive poems of this type are of course the two Anniversaries, written ostensibly to mourn the passing of Elizabeth Drury, but actually developing ingeniously and with elaborate cosmological reference, the **theme** of the "decay of the world" in his time.

Divine Poems

These consist chiefly of the *La Corona* poems (a sequence of seven sonnets, artfully woven together by **theme** and phrasing), translations from the Psalms, the nineteen *Holy **Sonnets*** (among which are the "Death be not proud" and "Batter my heart" sonnets), which contain some of Donne's most vivid **imagery** as well as his most genuine emotion, and a number of individual pieces, of which *Goodfriday, 1613. Riding Westward*, and the two Hymns (*To God the Father*, and *In my Sicknesse*) are the most enduring. At least one of the criteria by which Donne will probably continue to exceed Herbert and the other **metaphysical** poets in reputation, is his unquestioned mastery of both the love lyric and the short devotional poem.

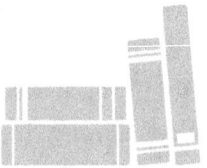

JOHN DONNE

THE ANNIVERSARY POEMS

The two Anniversaries are not only the most baffling productions of Donne's poetical career, but stand among the great curiosities of English literary history. The poems were occasioned by the death of Elizabeth Drury, the fifteen-year-old daughter of Sir Robert Drury, and were presumably composed by Donne with the design of eliciting the patronage of Sir Robert. As with so many "occasional" poems, Milton's *Lycidas* perhaps being the outstanding example, the Anniversaries thoroughly transcend the limited significance of a young girl's death, and provide Donne with the opportunity of putting into verse his sense of the break-up of the old world order, a vision which was fleshed out in terms of the enormous learning (truly encyclopedic) which Donne possessed. As complimentary verses to a girl Donne had never met, they ran the obvious risk of being regarded as fantastically extravagant in their praise, precisely what Jonson meant when he remarked that "if it had been written to the Virgin Mary it had been something."

THE FIRST ANNIVERSARY, AN ANATOMIE OF THE WORLD,

Wherein, by Occasion of the untimely death of Mistris Elizabeth Drury, the frailty and decay of this whole world is represented [1611]: The 474 lines of the poem fall naturally into seven parts: an introduction and an ending, with the middle (the "anatomy" proper) divided into five parts, the final section of each beginning with the words, "Shee, shee is dead; shee's dead: when thou knowest this, / Thou knowest how. . . ." This is then followed by a termination appropriate to the part of the anatomy being discussed.

Comment

There are three ideas entering into the basic fiction or **metaphor** of the poem:

1) The popular theory that the world was running down, and that it was now in its last age.

2) The macrocosm/microcosm conceit, which allows for the world to be treated here as a human body.

3) The meaning of an "anatomy," which was a public lecture in which the teaching doctor read from the works of Galen, while an assistant performed the dissection of the corpse.

The word "anatomy" was of course coming into use as a description of any sort of detailed written analysis, as, for instance, Burton's *Anatomy of Melancholy*.

Introduction (vv. 1 - 60): When that "rich Soule" (Elizabeth Drury's), like a Queen ending her journey through the realm, left for heaven, the world languished, its "vital spirits" being drawn out in the common tears of grief. It then began to suffer from an ague, which (on the mistaken notion that an ague, or shaking fit, was a means to health) caused men to think it well, when in fact it was in a "lethargy," having lost "sense and memory," as well as speech. "Her name defin'd thee, gave thee forme, and frame," and you (the World) have forgotten that name, thinking it "some blasphemy" to say she was dead. Since it is too late to attempt a cure of the world, its "intrinsic balm" being gone, the poet will see what can be gained by an anatomy.

First Division (vv. 61 - 190): Her death teaches that the world is "corrupt and mortal in [its] purest part," yet, even though by her death the World itself is dead, the anatomy is not useless, since her ghost still walks; that is, there is still a weak love of virtue and good, which is creating a new world from the carcass of the old. This new world can arm itself with the knowledge of danger and disease, and thus be made safer.

There is no health. Even in birth, children come head first and thus "fall upon an ominous precipitation." Woman, meant to be a helpmate for man, is the cause of his languishment, and having killed us all at one blow, they kill us singly, as "we will ourselves to propagate our kind" (intercourse shortens life). What has happened to that first age when man lived longer than stag or raven, and was great in size and absolutely erect in stature? Man is now "contracted to an inch, who was a spanne."

But this were light, did our lesse volume hold All the old Text; or had wee chang'd to gold Their silver; or dispos'd into lesse glasse Spirits of vertue, which then scatter'd was.

THE METAPHYSICAL POETS

Comment

This is a complicated set of images. First of all, there is a pun on the word "volume" (both book and volumetric capacity), but it seems also to suggest the relationship of the New and Old Testaments, on the principle (common in Biblical exegesis) that the New Testament, though shorter than the Old, is the fulfillment of it (hence, contains it all). Similarly, the silver of the post-Academic men (they lived in the Silver Age) might have become gold, which is not only more precious but more dense (hence, contains the same amount in less volume). So too with the "spirits of vertue," chemically (or alchemically) extracted from a greater mass, and thus concentrated.

But none of this is so. Our bodies and minds both are "cramped," and we seem to be trying to undo God's work. Man is now a trifle, and a poor thing, since "with her whom we lament, he lost his heart." She, in whom virtue was so much refined, who could drive out the poisonous tincture of sin, is gone.

Shee, shee is dead; shee's dead: when thou knowest this, Thou knowest how poore a trifling thing man is. And learn's thus much by our Anatomie, The heart being perish'd, no part can be free.

Comment

It was a commonplace of medieval and Renaissance medicine that the "heart dies last." (All the principal members of the body were thought of as separate entities, living and dying independently of the others). There is a certain fitness in this ending, since the main concern of the first part has been with "her virtue" and its role in preserving the frame of the world.

"Virtue" (L. virtus) in addition to its moral signification, had a meaning which referred to the efficacy arising from physical powers, and thus had close connections with the regulative power of the heart.

This part ends with an exhortation to man to "feed...on/ The supernatural food, Religion."

Second Division (vv. 191 - 248): This part begins with a reference to the world's whole frame being "Quite out of joynt, almost created lame," a form of corruption which began in the fall of the angels from grace, and ended by "Wronging each joynt of th'universall frame," man, beasts, and plants.

> Comment

This statement reflects the "great chain of being" motif, a typically classical and medieval concept (though it persisted long after), in which all things were arranged in an elaborate hierarchy according to their relative value in the scheme of the universe.

(Donne now illustrates the decay of the world in a passage which has often been quoted to illustrate his interest in the new science of his day. If we are to take the passage as a biographical fact, it shows Donne's interest to have been of a most reactionary sort).

And new Philosophy calls all in doubt, The Element of fire is quite put out; The Sun is lost, and the 'earth, and no man's wit Can well direct him where to looke for it. And freely men confesse that this world's spent, When in the Planets, and the Firmament They seeke so many new; they see that this Is crumbled out againe to his Atomies. 'Tis all in peeces, all cohaerence gone; All just supply, and all Relation:

Comment

"New Philosophy" refers primarily to the revolution in astronomical thought being wrought by the discoveries and publications of Copernicus, Kepler, and Galileo, but also to the new developments in mechanics which were to lead to Galileo's *Dialogues Concerning Two New Sciences* in 1638. The discovery of "new stars" (probably novae and comets) dealt the death blow to Aristotle's doctrine of the immutability of the celestial regions, while Copernicus' mathematical demonstration of the plausibility of taking the sun rather than the earth as the reference point of the celestial system was fast gaining adherents. The most astounding event of all, however, was Galileo's telescopical discovery in 1610 of the moons of Jupiter and of a host of stars of a magnitude not perceptible by the naked eye. It is probably best to think of Donne as merely using these discoveries as a **metaphor** for his "decay of the world" fiction rather than to condemn him as an obstructionist and reactionary.

He goes on to say that "she...had all Magnetique force alone,/ To draw, and fasten sundred parts in one," (an image based on William Gilbert's recent investigation of the properties of the lodestone, and his speculations about a magnetic field surrounding the earth itself [Gilbert's *De Magnete* was published in 1600]). She was a new compass for our world's voyage, a general steward to Fate, whose breath perfumed the East, and whose richness was the source of the gold of the Indies.

Shee, shee is dead; shee's dead: when thou knowst this, Thou knowst how lame a cripple this world is.

The world is suffering from a "Hectique feaver," which has warped it. To escape the general infection a man must be no part of the world.

Third Division (vv. 249 - 338): This section treats of the decay of the world's beauty - the loss of color and proportion. [Color is actually the subject of the next division.] This is seen in the invention of "eccentric parts" (to account for heavenly motions), the discovery of new stars, the substitution of elliptical for circular orbits, the precession of the equinoxes (Donne expresses this as the Sun moving with a "couzening line"), and a number of other departures from the hypothetical regularity and circularity of the old universe. The earth itself is not perfectly spherical, but marred by mountains (these were also thought to be a result of the Fall from grace). The world is disfigured, and the two legs it should rely on, reward and punishment, are "bent awry." She who was the measure of all symmetry and harmony, whose proportions must have been the pattern of the Ark itself, just as the Ark (in its harmonizing of contrarieties) must have been the pattern for her, "Shee, shee is dead, shee's dead; when thou knowst this,/ Thou knowst how ugly a monster this world is." To escape the general corruption a man must do things "fitly, and in proportion." Good [moral goodness] and well [functional aptness] must in our actions meet."

Fourth Division (vv. 339 - 376): Beauty's other element, color, is also spent. Sight is the noblest sense, yet it has only color to feed on, and that is all decayed. Even summer has grown dusky. This has occurred because "shee, in whom all white, and red, and blew/ (Beauties ingredients) voluntary grew," is dead. "Shee, shee is dead; shee's dead: when thou knowst this,/ Thou knowest how wan a Ghost this our world is." As a result it is now only "wicked vanity" to think that one may "colour vicious deeds with good pretence."

Fifth Division (vv. 377 - 434): The world's decay appears in nothing more pointedly than in the way that the heavens resist her "influence."

Comment

The stars and planets were thought to influence (from L. fluere, flow) earthly affairs, such as the nativity of an infant, on the supposition that there was a material nexus among all parts of the universe (a void being considered an impossibility) and that occult forces could "flow down" from heaven to earth. She, as the very world-soul itself, should thus be able to work an influence even on the celestial spheres, but they refuse to submit to it.

The clouds do not pour down rain, the air does not bring about seasonal progression, and the arts of divination and natural magic have been lost. Just as some poisons do not work unless they are shot directly from the serpent's mouth, so her virtue cannot work a cure without her presence to manifest it. "Shee, shee is dead, shee's dead; when thou knowst this / Thou knowst how drie a Cinder this world is." All our blood, sweat, and tears will not suffice to moisten it, in the absence of those "rich joyes, which did possesse her heart."

Conclusion (vv. 435 - 474): But the body scarcely lasts out the reading of the anatomy (before beginning to stink of corruption), so the poet must end his work. He asks the maiden to accept his tribute, and admonishes "her creatures" (all men) to take their "best concoction" (purifying process) "from her example, and her vertue." He apologizes for attempting to confine her merits in verse (since they deserve a chronicle), but justifies it on the ground that

Verse hath a middle nature: heaven keepes Soules, The Grave keepes bodies, Verse the Frame enroules.

THE SECOND ANNIVERSARY, OF THE PROGRESSE OF THE SOULE,

Wherein, by Occasion of the religious death of Mistris Elizabeth Drury, the incommodities of the soule in this life, and her exaltation in the next, are contemplated [1612]: This poem, like The *First Anniversary*, is divided (though without nearly the same degree of emphasis) into sections - an introduction, seven divisions, and a conclusion.

Comment

The title, *Of the Progresse of the Soule*, appears to blend three separate ideas:

1. The Christian doctrine that the souls of the just will rise to heaven after death, there to be re-united with their glorified bodies.

2. The Platonic theory that the soul after death rises upward, passing in turn through the several celestial spheres until it reaches its final resting place.

3. The contemporary meaning of "progress," as it refers to an official journey taken by a ruler through his provinces.

The soul is that of the poet, and the "progress" is its imaginary flight upward in emulation of the soul of Elizabeth Drury.

Introduction (vv. 1 - 44): Like the inertia which moves a ship after its sails have been struck, or like the grotesque motions made by the trunk and the head of a beheaded man, so this dead world is struggling now that she is gone. Since a new

Deluge, this time of the waters of Lethe (river of forgetfulness) has overtaken the world, the poet sees it as his task to bring forth hymns inspired by her, which will at least embalm (though they cannot revive the world, "till Gods great Venite change the song."

First Division (vv. 45 - 84): This section begins with the poet admonishing his soul to thirst for that time (the final Judgment Day) and forget this rotten world. That sort of stupidity and lethargy are really the best kind of alacrity and memory. Look upward her (Elizabeth Drury) whom we now congratulate rather than mourn. "Shee, shee is gone; when thou knowest this, / What fragmentary rubbidge this world is / Thou knowest...."

Second Division (vv. 85 - 156): This time the poet advises his soul to think itself on the deathbed, the "broken and soft Notes" of its laboring breath being in reality the "happiest Harmonie."

Comment

For several lines the poet labors the various aspects of the paradox involved in the fact that death is the beginning of eternal life. The looseness and slackness of the body is simply the unbinding of a pack so that the soul may be removed. The body's ague is actually its "Physick" (remedy). The death knell (sound of bells) is in fact a call to join the Church Triumphant. Satan's minions, thrusting about the body, are merely eager inheritors of the cardinal sins the body is leaving behind. (And more of the same.)

If the soul is "drowsy or slack" at that moment, it can think upon her perfect "complexion" (balanced combination of humors, betokening absolute health). Her "even constitution" repelled all disease. Her proportions were such that they made cubes appear unstable, and circles angular. Yet even she embraced a sickness, and thus serves as an example of the fact that a man with the surest title to heaven must be ushered into it by Death.

Third Division (vv. 157 - 250: The speaker next admonishes the soul to recall its poor beginnings, when it was "obnoxious" (that is, exposed to harm) and poisoned by the lump of flesh which it inhabited. The body was a prison-house, a poor Inn at most, a "province pack'd up in two yards of skin." In such a light, death has to be regarded as an enfranchisement, a new liberty, the hatching of the soul through a broken shell. As it flies through the heavens it does not concern itself with nice speculations about meteors, or the element of fire, but reaches at once for the Firmament and the sphere of the fixed stars, as if it were stringing beads in quick succession. But her fair body was no such prison, all the world's richest parts finding their counterparts in her, twenty times over, in fact. "Shee, shee, thus richly and largely hous'd, is gone," thus chiding us "slow-pac'd snailes" who remain behind.

Fourth Division (vv. 251 - 320): The fourth section opens with a rebuke to the soul for imagining that it really knows anything. It does not even know itself, having thought for ages that it was wrought of the four elements only to discover of late that there are other ingredients. It does not even know how blood travels from one ventricle to the other.

> Comment

Even Vesalius thought blood moved between the ventricles. Donne was of course writing some years before Harvey's celebrated lecture on the Circulation of the Blood, in which he demonstrated that the inter-ventricular septum was impermeable.

There follows a catalogue of elementary queries about which man has no certain knowledge, terminating in a scornful dismissal of telescopic investigation, and perhaps of the Baconian ideal of a collection of the phenomena of natural history ("nor learne ... by collections to discerne"). She, whose own thoughts surpassed libraries, and who was perfect in the art of "knowing Heaven," is gone. By taking herself she took away "our best, and worthiest booke."

Fifth Division (vv. 321 - 382): He asks the soul not to lose its ecstasy and reminds it that it will not find glib theologians, or libelling courtiers in heaven, but will listen to the song of angels, see the glory of the Blessed Virgin, and the joy of the prophets who are happy in the fulfillment of their prophecies. Among them, "shee" will be found, the very epitome of peace, beauty, chastity, and justice. She has left this sick world and has survived; and she should thus become an inspiration to others.

Sixth Division (vv. 383 - 470): The poet now reminds the soul that there is no essential joy upon earth, that all is transitory, and that happiness is a chance affair. The world has no more of a foundation for true joy than it had the material basis for the anticipated Tower of Babel. Only the beatific vision (the enduring vision of God in Heaven) is "essential joy." She, who, by her capacity for knowing God directly here on earth, had this "essential joy, even before death, is gone. Even heaven's accidental joys are greater than our "casual joys," and even in the midst of joy "casual violence" may strangle us.

Seventh Division (vv. 471 - 510): In heaven we find the paradox that "accidental things are permanent." Glorified bodies are capable of a new sort of joy:

This kind of joy doth every day admit Degrees of growth, but none of losing it.

But the concept of degree does her an injury, her "who left such a bodie, as even shee / Only in Heaven could learne, how it can be / Made better."

Conclusion (vv. 511 - 528): Here on earth the poet invokes the name of the maiden, calling his poem the work of Him "that gave thee power to doe, me, to say this."

Thou art the Proclamation; and I am The Trumpet, at whose voyce the people came.

SUMMARY

> The two Anniversaries are extravagant eulogies (the first is also an **elegy**, the second a hymn) of Elizabeth Drury, whom Donne has made the occasion for a sweeping analysis of his contemporary world. They are given a rigorously exact structure, the first rather more so than the second, a feature which may be explained by the fact that the first is a "mourning" poem, and demands a tighter control over the expression of grief, while the second is more of a "celebration" poem, and admits of a greater effusion of emotion, loftier flights of fancy, and a generally looser structure. (This may simply be a bit of ad hoc rationalization, however; the real reason for the difference might well be traced to the random workings of genius and inspiration.)

JOHN DONNE

SONGS AND SONNETS

THE INTENSITY OF LOVE

While most of the *Songs and **Sonnets*** are concerned with love in one form or another, there are a number which deal especially with the nature of the emotional relationship between the lovers, in particular the capacity of love to blot out considerations of time, space, and the ordinary demands of customs and society.

THE CANONIZATION

The speaker blurts out an impatient rebuke to some critic who objects to his being in love, and tells him to find some other occupation. He asks what harm his love has caused (what ships drowned by his sighs, estates inundated by his tears, spring seasons postponed by his chills, and plague victims struck down by his fevers).

> Comment

This is a sarcastic rejection of the exaggerated claims of sonneteers writing in the petrarchan tradition (an increasingly degenerate form of hyperbolical praise of a lady and itemization of the lover's pangs, deriving from Petrarch's **sonnet** sequence written to immortalize his beloved Laura).

The world goes about its business, the speaker maintains, even though they are in love, and he admits that the most unsavory **similes** may be applied to them (without reprehension, since it is love which makes them what they are). Let them be called "flies" (for blindly copulating?), or tapers, which at their "owne cost die" (that is, candles, burning but consuming themselves - based on a common pun on the word "die," which had a secondary meaning of "complete the sexual act," a meaning which was itself probably founded on the popular superstition that each instance shortened one's life by a day). The speaker can outdo his accusers in similes: "Eagle and the Dove" may be found in them (possibly a reference to voracious appetite and peaceful constancy, both of which are aspects of love); and the riddle of the Phoenix (the fabulous bird which produced its own successor from the ashes of its funeral pyre) finds an example in them, since they are two sexes accommodated "to one neutral thing," and

Wee dye and rise the same, and prove Mysterious by this love.

> Comment

Beneath the rather graphic physical accuracy of the image, there is an almost blasphemous level of religious **allusion**. The

Phoenix, of course, "dies and rises the same" in a myth which is a mystery in the ordinary sense, but it is impossible to escape the suggestion of the Crucifixion and Resurrection of Christ, which is a mystery in the proper religious sense, a sense insisted upon not only by the title ("canonization" means elevation to Christian sainthood), but by the marked religious vocabulary ("legends," "hymnes," "hermitage") which follows. Donne's witty **metaphor** finds its basis, and ultimately derives its meaning, however, from the fact that romantic love had for many years been treated in literature as a "religion," with its own god, saints, hymns, oratories, and so forth. (For a thorough analysis of this aspect of Courtly Love, see Chapter 1 of C. S. Lewis' *The Allegory of Love*.)

The speaker goes on to say that their "legend" (an account of a saint's miracles and exemplary deeds) will be fit for **sonnets** if not for chronicles, but that a "well wrought urne" (**sonnet**) befits the greatest ashes as finely as a "halfe-acre tombe" (chronicle), and that by these hymns (the **sonnets** written in their praise by succeeding generations of lovers) all men will recognize that they have been "Canoniz'd for Love." Future ages will "invoke" them (that is, ask them to intercede at the throne of the deity) as lovers

Who did the whole worlds soule contract, and drove Into the glasses of your eyes (So made such mirrors, and such spies, That they did all to you epitomize,) Countries, Townes, Courts: Beg from above A pattern of your love!

Comment

The "religion of love" figure is here complicated by the Platonic concepts of the world-soul (in Plato's *Timaeus* the physical world is regarded as a total organic, body with its own soul) and the celestial Ideas, or forms, which are the models ("pattern") for all earthly phenomena. Donne is suggesting, through **metaphor**, the intensity of a love which, by excluding all external considerations, in effect creates its own little world - the Idea or heavenly blueprint for which is worthy of being prayed for by all aspiring lovers. There is also a neat union of the physical and the abstract in the image of the lovers' eyes as "mirrors" (to be interpreted either as an optical device or as a Speculum, a common title for encyclopedic works) which "epitomize" (either bring rays of light to a focus, or gather together in summary form as in an encyclopedia) "Countries, Townes, Courts."

THE SUNNE RISING

This poem is a witty inversion of the tradition of the alba, or lover's complaint that the dawn forces him to leave his beloved. Donne eschews tender lyricism in favor of an impatient defiance of the sun, calling it a "busie old foole" and a "sawcy pedantique wretch," which should be about the business of awakening late schoolboys, disgruntled apprentices, and the king's huntsmen. The second **stanza** affirms the lover's superiority to the sun, whose beams he could eclipse with a mere wink, and goes on to prove with a specious show of logic that the lovers, by driving the whole world into their bedroom (through that intensity and egotistical exclusiveness of love), enjoy a full measure of happiness, while the sun, who must hence stand still to warm the "world" (now their room) only completes half of its assigned duty (that is, to warm both sides of the earth) and thus can be only half as happy as they.

Comment

There is a realistic aspect to the poem, in the fact that the intensity of love does, in fact, work to blot out all other considerations, but it is given metaphorical expression in the conceit that both the Indies (gold and aromatic spices), all States and Princes (the lady is a kingdom ruled by the lover), all honor and all wealth (their mutual respect and the sense of value their love imparts) - hence the entire world - is in their very room.

THE GOOD-MORROW

("Morrow" = "morning") The "good morning" is the greeting of the souls of the two lovers, now first awakening (as in the legend of the Seven Sleepers) to true pleasure from the fantasies of pleasure. The expansiveness of their genuine love has the effect of making "One little roome an everywhere," so that the lover can impugn the paltry efforts of discoverers and cartographers, whose "new worlds" cannot match the two worlds of the lovers ("each hath one, and is one").

Comment

That man is a microcosm, or "little world," analogous to the macrocosm, or "great world," is a commonplace medieval and Renaissance idea - one which Donne frequently employs. Thus, any aspect of the great world, such as the fact that the sun is the center and ruler of the cosmos, has its reverberation in the body of man (the heart is the sun of the microcosm, and provides vital nourishment to the blood, and so forth). Often, the earth itself is regarded as the macrocosm, producing such analogies as that between the course of rivers and the circulation of the blood.

The last **stanza** makes the microcosm **metaphor** more specific by suggesting that the lovers' faces are reflected in each other's eyes, resulting in two perfect hemispheres, lacking "sharp North" and declining West," and thus not susceptible to death.

LOVERS INFINITENESS

The poet here plays upon the Aristotelian definition of the infinite as "that of which, however much you have taken, there is always more to take," and the related idea that "that from which something, no matter what, is missing and left outside is not 'All'." So in the first **stanza** the lover acknowledges that since the lady's gift of love was only "partial" (since, in her fickleness, she may have reserved some of her love for others) he can never have her "All." In the second, he considers the possibility that she has given him all her love (by making her original gift of love "general"), and in the third begins by refusing to accept "all," since his own love growing day by day should find no correspondingly new love in the lady; but he ends on the optimistic note that they have a "way more liberal" (presumably, sexual union) than the Platonic "exchange of hearts," and that this, by making them "one another's all," gives them each a new sort of infiniteness.

THE ANNIVERSARY

The occasion is the first anniversary of the lovers' original sight of one another. All things draw towards their destruction except their love, which has no yesterday or tomorrow. In death they must leave their bodies behind, but their souls, "where nothing dwells but love," will continue to be the repositories of love. They will then "be thoroughly blest" but "no more than all the rest."

Comment

The point of the **metaphor** rests upon the theological doctrine that all of the souls in heaven will enjoy complete happiness, the fullest measure they are capable of sustaining. Thus, one may not be said to be more blessed than another.

This notion leads the speaker to consider how, then, they may achieve any uniqueness, and he decides that it is here on earth, where they are kings - where, in fact, only they can be such kings and such subjects (since they are king and subject to each other). Therefore, he says,

Let us live nobly, and live, and adde againe Yeares and yeares unto yeares, till we attaine To write threescore: this is the second of our raigne.

THE FLEA

The lover is using the flea which has just bitten both himself and the lady as an argument in favor of her yielding herself to him. It is based upon the conceit that their "bloods are mingled" in the flea, and that this is therefore no different from the "mingling of bloods" which would result from their union; there is no "sinne, nor shame, nor losse of maidenhead." The lady is about to kill the flea, but the lover points out that the flea is now (a) both of them, (b) their marriage bed, and (c) their marriage temple, and that she is about to commit murder, suicide, and sacrilege. By the last **stanza** it is apparent that the lady has killed the flea, and she claims that she finds that neither of them has been weakened by it, to which the lover replies:

'Tis true, then learne how false, feares bee; Just so much honor, when thou yeeld'st to mee, Will wast, as this flea's death tooke life from thee.

A NOCTURNAL UPON S. LUCIES DAY, BEING THE SHORTEST DAY

This fine tender expression of love is in the form of a meditation for nocturn (one of the divisions of matins, the part of the daily canonical hours usually recited at midnight). Since the feast of St. Lucy occurred around the time of the winter solstice it is also the "yeares midnight." The sun is spent, the sap of the world has sunk into the ground, and the speaker is lying on his bed, so drained of life (and hence flattened) that he seems to be the "**epitaph**" for the general interment of the world. In the second **stanza** the poet calls upon lovers to study his case as an example of the way in which Love totally ruins his devotees. Love has wrought a new kind of alchemy, in which the poet has been made the quintessence of nothingness.

Comment

Alchemists sought to produce the Elixir, or Philosopher's Stone by seeking for the quintessence (fifth, or celestial, essence) which they hoped to extract from a bewildering variety of substances by separating it from the four basic elements of which they were composed. The witty turn here is that Love, as Alchemist, does not extract the quintessence from things but from nothings, such as privation, emptiness, absence, darkness, and death.

The poet refers to himself as being treated in "love's limbeck" (that is, the alembic, or alchemical vessel) until he becomes the Elixir produced out of the "first nothing," and (because of the death of his beloved) is completely devoid of properties. He bids other lovers "enjoy your summer all," but as for himself,

Let mee prepare towards her, and let me call This houre her Vigill, and her Eve, since this Both the yeares, and the dayes deep midnight is.

The Nocturnall is an impressive blend of tender sentiment, alchemical **imagery**, and hackneyed Petrarchan conceits based on the "religion of love," to produce a poem which conveys a poignant sense of genuine love and personal desolation.

THE EXTASIE

The punning title of *The Extasie* refers not only to the rapturous silence of two lovers in mutual contemplation, but to departure of their souls from the bodies (from Gr. ekstasis, displacement). The speaker recalls how they sat:

Our hands were firmly cimented With a fast balme, which thence did spring, Our eye-beames twisted, and did thred Our eyes, upon one double string;

So far, the reflections in each other's eyes was all that they had propagated. Their souls, like negotiators of a truce, had gone forth, leaving the bodies "like sepulchrall statues:" yet, so pure were they, that they spoke exactly the same, yet not so pure that by mingling they could not be made even stronger

> When love, with one another so Interinanimates two soules,
> That abler soule, which thence doth flow, Defects of lonelinesse controules.

[That is, the new soul formed by the union of the first two cures any defects they suffered from singly.]

But even pure lovers' souls must return to their bodies, in which weak lovers (reading them like a book which reveals religious mysteries) will see "small change, when we'are to bodies gone" (that is, union and ecstasy will be as characteristic of the lovers' bodies as their souls).

THE RELIQUE

This is probably addressed to Lady Magdalen Herbert, and is concerned with the pure Platonic love they shared. The poet looks ahead to the day when his grave will be broken up and the workmen, spying "a bracelet of bright hair about the bone," might bring these to the Bishop and King then reigning as relics to be preserved, if it is a time when "mis-devotion doth command."

Comment

The bracelet of hair is a love momento sent by the lady to the man. That is her relic and the bone is his. Mis-devotion refers, of course, to a perversion of religion, a time when sinners are regarded as saints.

She will thus be revered as a Mary Magdalene, and he as "a something else." The miracles expected of them are the miracles the poet is now going to record (and here the poem takes a witty turn, establishing that they were "harmless lovers," who were not even aware of a difference of sex). The only kisses they permitted each other were legitimate kisses of salutation. This was miracle enough, but "all measure, and all language" would have to be surpassed for the poet to tell what a "miracle" she was.

TWICKNAM GARDEN

The poem may be addressed to Lucy, Countess of Bedford; if so, it is an exaggerated compliment to the lady, based on the fiction that the poet has brought seductive love into her garden and that by her "truth" (to her marriage vows) she is killing him. Overcome by sighs and tears, he begins, he has come to the garden for a healing balm. But he has brought "the spider love," and that it may truly be thought "True Paradise, I have the serpent brought." (Paradoxically, the Garden of Eden is not Paradise without the serpent, but it is the serpent which brings sin and death into it.) The very beauty of the place mocks his love, he complains, and so that he should not have to endure this disgrace nor yet leave loving, he implores Love to make him a mandrake or a stone fountain, whose tears lovers may use to test the genuineness of their own lady's tears (since eyes alone cannot be trusted). This leads to the witty, paradoxical ending,

O perverse sexe, where none is true but shee, Who's therefore true, because her truth kills me.

THE NATURE OF LOVE AND ITS EFFECTS IN THE INDIVIDUAL

In a number of lyrics Donne is concerned more with the psychological and physiological results of love in the single person than with love as a relationship or as a social phenomenon. Of course, this is a very hazy distinction, but we do note several poems in which the speaker, in solitary contemplation, attempts to analyze his feelings.

LOVES GROWTH

It is spring, and the lover reflects that his love can hardly be as pure or as infinite as he imagined since, like grass, it has endured the winter season and come up stronger than before. (If absolutely pure it could not change, and if infinite it could not increase. Love is not so pure and abstract as poets say, but is elemented (mixed with matter).

Comment

The problem to be resolved through **metaphor** is that of "proving" that love is pure - of showing, by some sort of witty paradox, that the "growth" in his love is neither augmentation nor change. The second **stanza** does just this.

By springtime, he decides, his love has not grown greater but "more eminent," just as stars (as it was thought) are not enlarged but only "shown" by the sun. Love's additions are not more a "growth" than the circles produced by a disturbance in the water, nor do they multiply that love any more than the several celestial spheres make up more than one heaven.

And though each spring doe adde to love new heate, As princes doe in times of action get New taxes, and remit them not in peace, No winter shall abate the springs encrease.

THE DREAME

The speaker has been awakened from a dream by a vision of his beloved, and addresses her as if she were actually there, continuing in reality what was a moment before only dream fantasy. This conceit is based on the assertion that she is "so truth" that mere thoughts of her can make dreams truths, and fables histories. It was the light from her eyes that awakened him, and when he realized that by coming at the precise moment that she did she must have had the power (which even an angel does not have) of reading his thoughts, then he knew that it would be "Prophane, to thinke thee anything but thee." [That is, she is a deity, in whom (as Grierson notes) essence and existence are one. All one can really predicate of God is that He is.]

Rising from his bed, the poet begins to doubt her real presence, and decides that she must be dealing with him as those do who light torches when they have to be kept in readiness, and then extinguish them.

Thou cam'st to kindle, goest to come; Then I Will dreame that hope againe, but else would die.

LOVES DEITIE

The poet wishes he could speak with the ghost of some lover who died before the god of Love was born, so that he might confirm his belief that no man then loved a woman who did not return his love.

But since this god produc'd a destinie, And that vice-nature, custome, lets it be; I must love her, that loves not mee.

Comment

This is all a reference to the pure **convention** (going back to the very origins of Courtly Love in the Middle Ages) that a lover must languish and a lady remain disdainful for as long as she wished. Donne playfully pretends that it is a decree of the god of Love, and then proceeds to analyze and question the domain which Love exercises over his devotees.

Neither those who defied him, nor Love himself (in the beginnings of his reign), ever intended any more than "correspondencie," the union of suitable actives and passives. Love, if it is really love, involves mutuality. But modern gods have become tyrants, and men should "ungod this child again" (referring pointedly to Love not as the commanding figure of Eros, but as the child Cupid). Finally, the speaker decides that he had best cease complaining, since he fears that Love might react by making him "leave loving" (which he is unwilling to do) or by forcing her to love him (which would be an act of falsehood, since she already loves another).

Falsehood is worse than hate; and that must be, If shee whom I love, should love mee.

LOVES DIET

Love is introduced in the first **stanza** as some sort of pet, which has grown fat and has to be slimmed down by being put on a diet of discretion. He was allowed one sigh a day from his master (none from the lover's mistress, whose sighs the lover reveals to be unsound), and one of this master's tears "brin'd with scorn" (the mistress' tears were all counterfeit, he was informed). By such means the lover "reclaimed" his "buzard love" (a buzzard being a useless kind of hawk), and now, like any negligent falconer,

I spring a mistresse, sweare, write, sigh and weepe: And the game kill'd, or lost, goe talke, and sleepe.

["Spring" = causes a bird to rise from cover. The lover, that is, is now like any heart-free gallant.]

THE CYNIC'S VOICE

There is a cynical tone to a great many of Donne's poems, *Love's Diet* being as good an example as most. There are several lyrics, however, which address themselves explicitly to the matter of the ephemeral quality of love, or the specious allurements of women, and in general adopt an air of ironic resignation to an essentially imperfect sort of relationship.

THE BAITE

The poem is one of numerous seventeenth-century "replies" to Christopher Marlowe's *The Passionate Shepherd to his Love*, which begins (like Donne's) "Come live with me and be my love," but goes on to catalogue the totally innocuous pleasures such as embroidering skirts with "leaves of myrtle" and other chaste delights which Marlowe's shepherd proposes to his paramour. Donne opens his version,

Come live with me, and bee my love, And we will some new pleasures prove Of golden sands, and christall brookes, With silken lines, and silken hookes.

He then describes the avidity with which fish will run to the lady as she swims, more eager to catch her than she to catch them, and compares her (to their disadvantage) with anglers who freeze, injure themselves, and busy themselves making "curious traitors, sleavesilke flies" to bewitch the wandering eyes of poor fishes, ending the comparison thus:

For thee, thou needst no such deceit, For thou, thy selfe art thine owne bait; That fish, that is not catch'd thereby, Alas, is wiser farre than I.

THE FUNERALL

Donne admonishes the person (whoever he might be) who comes to shroud him, not to question "that subtile wreathe of haire, which crowns my arme." It is, of course, a bracelet made of his lady's hair, and the poet explains that it is his outward soul, which may serve to keep his body from dissolution when his own proper soul has left it. "If the sinewie thread my brain lets fall / Through every part" (that is, the soul, conceived of as a network of filaments descending from the brain) can unify him into a single person, why should not those hairs which grow upward from a better brain (that is, the bracelet made of his lady's hair) do it even better, unless she meant it as a manacle rather than a love token. In any case, he concludes, let it be buried with him; though it bespoke some humility on his part to accord it the qualities of a soul, "So, 'tis some bravery, That since you would save none of me, I bury some of you."

["Bravery" (here) = fit, ironic retribution. Since he, as a typical Petrarchan lover, was a victim of the lady's disdain, it is fitting that a part of her be buried with him.]

THE BLOSSOME

This poem is a witty inversion of a traditional "debate of the body and soul," in which each berates the other for the person's condemnation to hell. In the first **stanza** the speaker muses upon the fate of a blossom which little realizes that though now it triumphs on the bough, tomorrow it will be fallen. The second **stanza** says much the same thing to the heart, which hopes to make the lady yield through a long siege, but which is destined to accompany its owner to London on the next day. The speaker then pretends that the heart, which likes to be "subtile to plague thy selfe," will refuse to go, on the ground that the poet is going to visit friends who are concerned only to provide for his body. The poet jocularly agrees to let the heart remain, but advises it that the lady, having no heart herself, will not recognize it.

Practise may make her know some other part, But take my word, shee doth not know a Heart.

He finally directs the heart to meet him in London in twenty days, when it will find him fresher and fatter by being with men.

For God's sake, if you can, be you so too: I would give you There, to another friend, who wee shall finde As glad to have my body, as my minde.

THE TRIPLE FOOLE

The poet begins with a blunt acknowledgment that he is two fools, for falling in love and for writing poetry about it. He implies that the hope of winning his beloved keeps him in love, and declares that he thought to allay his pains by "fettering" them in verse (on the principle that composition of poetry is a kind of therapy). But no sooner has he done, than some musician sets his words to music and sings them to the delight of many, thus increasing his love and grief, and making him (through their publication) a third fool, who was before only two.

Comment

This is of course a song, and as such is much simpler in conception and structure, as well as more regular and smooth in verse form and rhythm than lyrics not intended to be sung.

AGAINST WOMEN

All of the poems in the preceding section are, of course, in some fashion and to some extent "against women," but there are several others which declare against the fair sex with such vehemence or venom that they become a poetry of abuse or invective rather than **irony**. This is not to say that Donne himself subscribed to the statements made by the poems but only that the speaker in the immediate dramatic situation presents himself as a misogynist.

LOVES ALCHYMIE

Comparing love to the will-o'-the wisp quest of the alchemists for the all-powerful Elixir, the poet asserts that he has never been able, and will never be able, to find "that hidden mysterie." It is all imposture, and just like the alchemists, lovers hope for a "rich and long delight" but get only a "winter-seeming summers night." Why should men give up everything for this "vaine Bubles shadow?" Even the Platonist, who swears that it is a marriage of minds that he seeks with a woman is doomed to disappointment:

Hope not for minde in women; at their best Sweetnesse and wit,
they'are but Mummy, possesst.

> Comment

This closing **couplet** is an excellent illustration of the density of Donne's thought (reflected both in verbal ambiguity and in syntactical looseness) and of the often praised use of "organic **metaphor**" (that is, a consistent application of an analogy which is not detachable from the poem and which is not complete until the poem is complete. The first point to be noted is the ambiguity of the word "Mummy"; it refers both to the Egyptian mummy (hence a mindless, spiritless body) and to the alchemical ingredient mumia (so called because it was originally derived from mummies, though later it was an ersatz substance produced by local entrepreneurs). "Possesst" may also refer either to simple possession (as when a man possesses a woman in marriage) or to diabolical "possession" (when a demonic spirit inhabits a human personality). This ambiguity in the word "possest" is emphasized by the comma following "Mummy," just as there is an ambiguity or uncertainty of response caused by the lack of a comma after "best." The reader may work out all the possible combinations of meaning these considerations entail, but the central fact to bear in mind is that all of these meaning are in one way or another the fulfillment of potentialities established in the images of the opening lines.

SONG ("GOE, AND CATCHE A FALLING STARRE")

The first **stanza** demands that the listener attempt a number of impossible things, "catch a falling star," "get with child (that is, make pregnant) a mandrake root," for instance, each seeming more fantastic than the preceding, but culminating in the imperative (from its final position, seeming the most fantastic of all):

And finde What winde Serves to advance an honest minde.

The second **stanza** deals in a similar fashion with all the "strange wonders" the listener might encounter on a trip around the world, and insists that the traveler will "sweare" / Nowhere / Lives a woman true, and faire" (that is, beauty makes it impossible for a woman to be true). The final stanza allows as a hypothesis that one such woman might be found, but concludes:

Yet shee Will bee False, ere I come, to two, or three.

Comment

It is obvious that the effect of this poem cannot be fully achieved in a rapid reading, but requires the slow deliberateness of song, which allows for the build-up of suspense and the pleasure of surprise.

WOMANS CONSTANCY

The speaker begins by stating as a foregone conclusion that his beloved (of one day) will of course jilt him the next day, and he proposes the specious arguments she might use to justify her inconstancy: Pretend that a new vow was actually made some time before; that they are not the same persons (since the material of the body undergoes change) they were before; that oaths taken in fear (of the wrath of the god of Love) are not binding; that since death ends true contracts, sleep ends lovers' contracts (only images of the former); or, that the lady, having made change the principle of her life, can only be true (to herself) through falsehood (to him). He could easily refute these sophistries, the speaker maintains, but he would rather not, since tomorrow he may believe them himself.

ON SEPARATION

These "valediction" poems ("valediction" of course, means, a farewell) deal with the effects on each of the lovers of their parting, and with the ways in which they can overcome the results of separation. This is frequently only a witty "proof" that they are not really separated at all. Since Donne made frequent journeys abroad and within England, it is likely enough that there may have been a real leave-taking as the occasion for some of the poems.

A VALEDICTION: FORBIDDING MOURNING.

Just as at the death of virtuous men there is little show of grief, so let us part, declares the speaker, in silence. For just as the "trepidation of the spheres" does not raise nearly as great an outcry as "moving of the earth" (probably a reference to ominous predictions of future disasters portended by earthquakes), so their "refined love" is less dependent upon the physical senses than the "elemental love" of "dull sublunary lovers." Their united souls cannot be broken but only endure an expansion "like gold to ayery thinnesse beate" or like the two legs of a pair of compasses. (This is perhaps the most famous example of the metaphysicals' so-called "farfetched" **imagery**):

If they be two, they are two so As stiffe twin compasses are two, Thy soule to fixt foot, makes no show To move, but doth, if the'other doe.

The lady's firmness draws his circle justly, and "makes me end, where I begunne."

A VALEDICTION: OF WEEPING

As the lovers weep at their parting, the speaker notices that his own tears are not only coined by her (that is, she is the cause of them), but they bear her stamp (reflect her image as he looks at them). This makes them "pregnant" of her (recalling the similarity of tear-shaped to womb-shaped), and make them "fruits of much griefe" (now pear-shaped and falling, as a ripe fruit) and "emblemes of more" (that is, pictorial symbols suggesting a richness of meaning behind them). But when a tear falls, then "that thou" falls and puts the speaker and his beloved on opposite shores. The second **stanza** compares each tear to a globe-blank, it is nothing, but when the continents (her image) are pasted on it becomes All (the world). In the last, he implores the lady not to drown him (like the Moon she causes the flood tide) with tears, nor to suck forth his spirit with her sighs and thus hasten his death.

A VALEDICTION: OF MY NAME IN THE WINDOW

Before leaving, the lovers scratches his name in a window with a diamond; his name thus imparts his firmness to the window (that is, gives it the hardness of diamond) while the lady's eye, looking at the name, will give it the value of diamond. But since glass is both transparent and reflective, the lady will see through him (his name) while she also sees her own reflection, and they will be the same ("I am you"). The name will remain with her unchanged (a sign of his constancy,), but what is more, she will have his very "pattern" (that is, his soul) with her continually. If this is too profound a meaning to impute to "a scratch'd name" she may keep it in any case as a "death's head (a memento mori, or reminder of man's mortality). Or, she may regard "this ragged bony name" as his "ruinous Anatomie" (his skeleton).

Then, as all my soules bee, Emparadis'd in you, (in whom alone I understand, and grow and see,) The rafters of my body, bone Being still with you, the Muscle, Sinew, and Veine, Which tile this house, will come againe.

Comment

Man was thought to have three souls, rational (understand), vegetative (grow), and sentient (see). Thus, since his souls are with her ("emparadis'd"), and his bones (the name in the window) are also at hand, a paradisal act, like that creative act of God which made Eve from Adam's rib, will provide "muscle, sinew, and veine."

Stanzas 6 and 7 then interpret the "engraved characters" as those mystical signs used by astrologers to call down celestial influences, and since they were inscribed when "love and griefe their exaltation [ascendancy] had," the lady should not resist the influences (love and sadness) but "daily mourne" for him. **Stanza** 8 alludes to the possibility that the lady may admit a new lover (open the casement window to him), and warns her that the "trembling" name (in the shaking window frame) betokens the living spirit of the speaker, offended by the lady's inconstancy. The ninth expresses the hope that the engraved name may "hide" any other lover's name (on a letter), the tenth that it may direct the lady's thought (whomever she may intend to write to) him. "But," he concludes,

... glasse, and lines must bee No meanes our firme substantiall love to keepe;

And he begs to be excused for his idle talk, since "dying men talke often so."

SUMMARY

It is obvious that there is a great deal of miscellaneous technical information in Donne's poems, contributing to their difficulty, not to mention the recondite academic learning, the traditional literary conventions, and the occasional references to the "new philosophy," that changing picture of the universe being wrought by the discoveries of men like Copernicus, Kepler, and Galileo. Following are a number of topics that recur often in the *Songs and Sonets*:

1. The Religion of Love: This was a partly literary and partly social game which went back (through such famous poems as the *Roman de la Rose*) to the "courts of love" in medieval Provence and to the poetry of the troubadours, not to mention the famous and basic document, *The Art of Courtly Love*, written in the late twelfth century by Andreas Capellanus for Marie, the daughter of Eleanor of Aquitaine. The assumptions were that there was a god of Love presiding over a religious system in which woman was idealized and man was her willing servant, doing her constant bidding, importuning for her favors, and writing

poetic persuasions to love. The lady was always obdurate and disdainful ("daungerous"), the lover was ever languishing, sighing, weeping, and prone to alternate bouts of fever and chill, though always keeping his love secret. This "religion" had its own rites, prayers, saints, and so forth; there is even a surviving medieval poem known as *The Lover's Mass*. Donne's *The Canonization* is a weary rejection of all the inane posturing of courtly lovers, and a plea for a more realistic vision of the relationship between men and women. In *The Dampe* the lovers' anatomies will show the lady's Disdain and Honor, and the lover's Constancy and Secretness. In *The Indifferent*, the lover is called a heretic by Venus for imagining that men and women can ever be faithful to one another. A *Valediction Of the Booke* alludes to "Loves Divines," that is, theologians in the religion of Love, who can make their "biblical exegesis" on "this book" (the lovers' collected letters), instead of the Bible. Love's *Deity* makes the relationship between the god of Love and his devotees a basic **metaphor**. In short, Donne is given to constant and familiar references to this **convention**, but always with a witty cynicism.

2. Petrarchanism: Petrarch took over the entire machinery of Courtly Love, and pressed it into the service of a poetry which insisted that love was a spiritualizing force and an ennobling experience for the man, and which proceeded to idealize woman even further. Petrarch's **imagery** became the subject of countless imitations, finally becoming fixed in sterile comparisons of the lady's eyes to stars, her forehead to ivory, her hair to gold (she was always blonde in the lover's poems), and so forth. The

tradition had worn itself out long before 1600, though contemporary poetasters were still grinding them out. Shakespeare rejects the entire paraphernalia of Petrarchanism in his **sonnet** beginning "My mistress' eyes are nothing like the sun," and Donne does much the same in such poems as *The Indifferent*, in which he claims to be able to "love both faire and browne" (that is, both blondes and brunettes, or possibly both fair-skinned and sunburned ladies). In "Negative Love" he abjures the techniques of those poets who stoop as low as to prey on an eye, cheek, or lip (the superficial Petrarchans) as well as those who "soare no higher then vertue or the minde to' admire" (the more ethereal or Platonic sorts).

3. Popular conception of woman: Another traditional attitude toward women, growing out of the suspicious or neurotic visions of some medieval moralists, and traceable to the traumatic racial experience of the Garden of Eden, saw deceit, instability, and inconstancy as woman's essential characteristics. When this attitude fell together with the image of woman's love as a fortress to be subdued, derived from the Roman de la Rose, there grew up a literary fashion centering on woman's fickleness. Wyatt, earlier in the sixteenth century, is a good example of this, as in his "They flee from me that sometime did me seek," though it was clearly discernible even in Chaucer's day. The special vocabulary associated with this attitude comes into Donne's poetry continually. Some examples:

a. "Kind": This originally meant "Nature" (hence "natural"), but began to shade over into its current meaning early enough for a poet like Wyatt to suggest ironically that his lady is being "unkind" (to him) even while she is "kind" (acting according to her womanly nature). The same sort of playing upon the idea is seen in Donne's Song, "Sweetest love, I do not goe":

> When thou sigh'st, thou sigh'st not winde, But sigh'st my soule away, When thou weep'st, unkindly kinde, My lifes blood doth decay.

b. "Inconstancy" (also "change," "variety"): In *The Indifferent*, Donne represents Venus as chiding "poor heretics in love" who "think to stablish dangerous constancy." Inconstancy was woman's prerogative.

c. "Deceit" (also "untruth," "Falsehood"): *The Song*, "Goe and catch a falling starre" is based on this idea, as is *The Baite*.

It is a prevalent **theme** with Donne, whole poems (like *Woman's Constancy*) centering on it, as well as single images, as in *The Legacie*, in which the lady's heart is thus described:

> It was not good, it was not bad, It was entire to noe, and few had part... But oh, no man could hold it, for 'twas thine.

4. Platonism: Plato's philosophy stressed the insubstantiality of the visible world, the necessity for escaping from the prisonhouse of the fleshly body, and the superiority of intellectual and spiritual relationships to mere involvement of the senses. The chief Elizabethan literary manifestations of Platonism were the motifs of the "marriage of minds" as superior to physical union, the idea that true lovers' souls could unite even when the bodies were separated (the conceit of the "exchange of hearts" being a modification of this). Such poems as *Loves Alchymie*, which refers to "that loving wretch that sweares, / 'Tis not the bodies marry, but the mindes," or *Lovers Infiniteness*, which pointedly declares that these true lovers (suffering no delusions about the spiritual aspect of love) "will have a way more liberall, / Than changing hearts, to joyne them." Donne uses Platonic conventions, but almost always with the effect of asserting the greater reality of sense experience, or, perhaps more accurately, the necessity of realizing that love is a personal, not merely a spiritual relationship.

5. The "old science": The world picture up to Donne's day was to a great extent a popularization of the ideas about the universe, the animal kingdom, and the body of man inherited from classical thinkers, notably Aristotle and Galen. Academic theorists continued to analyze and comment on these authors, and long after the discoveries of men like Copernicus and Harvey the medieval world picture continued to influence man's imaginative grasp of the physical world. Donne, without showing an absolute commitment to Aristotelian science, uses

its doctrines as the bases for many of his metaphors. Some of the chief concepts:

a. The geocentric universe: The earth was at the center of a closed, spherical system (containing, variously, from eight to eleven concentric spheres), in which spheres of water, air, and fire immediately surrounded the earth (these are the four "elements"), and were succeeded by the spheres of the Moon, Sun, the five known planets, the firmament of the fixed stars, a crystalline sphere, and a final sphere called the primum mobile (prime mover). There are countless references to this system in Donne's poetry. In *A Valediction: Of Weeping*, for instance, he addresses the lady,

O more than Moone Draw not up seas to drowne me in thy spheare.

b. Generation and corruption: All things in the sphere of the moon and beyond were not subject to accidental motion or to decay; all things below (in the "sublunary" world) were. The Dissolution begins: "Shee' is dead; And all which die / To their first Elements resolve." *A Valediction: Forbidding Mourning* alludes to the "trepidation of the spheres" and goes on to explain that "dull sublunary lovers love / (Whose soule is sense) cannot admit / Absence, because it doth remove / Those things which elemented it."

c. Macrocosm and microcosm: This goes back further than Aristotle (who mentions the idea with respect), and it was developed by medieval thinkers to the point at which all conceivable aspects of the great world were mirrored in the little world of man (and even, though this was not so widespread, in the geocosm or globe). Thus in *A Feaver* we read: "These burning fits but meteors bee, / Whose matter in thee is soone. spent. / Thy beauty, 'and all parts, which are thee, / Are unchangeable firmament. "For the microcosm/geocosm analogy, see Loves Alchymie; "Some that have deeper digged love's mine than I / Say, where his centrique happiness doth lie."

There are of course numerous other ancient "scientific" ideas to be found in Donne's poetry, such as the Platonic doctrine of the world-soul (see A Feaver: "Or if, when thou, the worlds soule, goest, / It stay, 'tis but thy carkasse then"), and the principle that "nature abhors a vacuum" (see *The Broken Heart;* "Yet nothing can to nothing fall, / Nor any place be empty quite"). What is proved by all of this is that Donne had a wide fund of the sort of academic learning one might acquire at the universities and that he drew upon it frequently for his metaphors.

6. Rhetoric and scholastic argument: Training in disputation was part and parcel of a Renaissance education; it was still to a great extent dominated by the techniques of the Schoolmen - what, in Bacon's view, was nothing else than logic-chopping and hairsplitting. Paradoxes, specious syllogistic proofs,

and tortuous arguments about the natures of things not observable by the senses, were the hallmarks of scholastic argument in its decline. Bacon appreciated to some extent the great power of mind that went into a medieval theoretical treatise (like the *Summa Theologia of St. Thomas Aquinas*) but Donne seems to have ended with little but contempt for the Schoolmen, though their influence on his thought is everywhere apparent. *Lovers Infinitenesses* is in one sense a scholastic quibble based on Aristotelian theories of the "All" and the "Infinite." "Aire and Angells" makes the qualitative difference between the purity of angelic substance and that of air the criterion for discriminating between the love of men and that of women.

In *The Dreame* he makes use of the scholastic distinction between essence and existence. In *A Lecture Upon the Shadow* he tortures the analogy between the changing dimensions of a shadow and the variability of human love in the manner of a formal scholastic lecture. But these are merely a few specific instances of a tendency, to pun, quibble, and employ remote analogies which is everywhere in the poetry and which was to a high degree conditioned by his scholastic training.

It would of course be wrong to leave a reader with the impression that the *Songs and **Sonnets*** are little more than an intellectual tour de force, and that their interest is mainly as a repository of archaic learning and a monument to perverse wit. There is a feeling as well as a thinking person behind the poems, and while one cannot construct a coherent picture of a developing life, or analyze the progress of a growing sensibility, it is nevertheless true that real love, real sorrow and disappointment, as well as gaiety and humor shine through the poetry. It must always be remembered that the *Songs and* **Sonnets** were not written for publication, but intended for the private delectation of a group of people whose interests were congenial to Donne's. The facts will simply not support the claim that Donne's verse is unrhythmical, any more than they give credence to the complaint that he "perplexed the minds of the fair sex" with philosophical speculations. The rhythms are carefully adjusted to the flow of the thought, with its many qualifications, and the thoughts are those which must certainly have appealed to the very sophisticated circle of which Donne was a part.

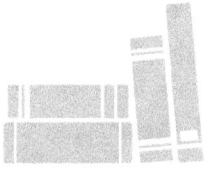

JOHN DONNE

ELEGIES

These poems are not elegies in the strict sense, but verses based on the love poems of Ovid, mistakenly referred to in the Renaissance as his *Elegies*. They are characterized by a jaunty and penetrating wit - a saucy nonchalance - with caustic and satirical thrusts throughout. One example should suffice.

ELEGIE XII: HIS PARTING FROM HER.

This poem of 104 lines is not divided into stanzas, nor is there any other formal sort of structure. Its structure is purely a matter of consistent internal development. In general, the subject of the poem is a lover's complaint that he must leave his beloved, and his imaginative search for a way to reconcile himself (and her) to their parting. The energy which moves the poem along is the speaker's impatience with Love, all of whose requirements they have carried out punctiliously, yet without the peaceful and permanent union they desire.

The speaker begins by challenging Night to come and try to impart a darkness greater than that of the inner Hell which is his, in the absence of his love. He could lend the Night such additional darkness that there would be no more day, did not the "fires within" (that is, the fires of love) "force a light." How, he asks, can fire and darkness be so mixed, and how can the "triumphs" of love be attended by such torments. Have they left undone "some mutual Rite?" (The machinery of the Religion of Love is of course responsible for many of the images in the poem.) But no, he says, the fault was his own, or at least to be imputed to "conspiring destinie," which decided to make him suffer, now that he was really in love, for all his former purely perfunctory loving. Yet why should his beloved also be made to suffer Love's wrath? Was it not enough that they bore mutually all the sighs, tears, and fevers of love? That they had to put up with secrecy, and with fear of a husband's jealousy? Were they not constant through all of this, maintaining their spies, their secret correspondence, their subtle gestures of recognition? Must divorce finally be their end? Before that should happen, let them be so united that blind Fortune, striving to separate them, shall have her eyes strained open and made bloody. Love itself could not be guilty of this mischief.

He challenges Fortune to do her worst:

Rend us in sunder, thou canst not divide Our bodies so, but that our souls are ty'd, And we can love by letters still and gifts, And thoughts and dreams; Love never wanteth shifts.

All things will remind him of their love: the Sun will suggest her beauty; the various elements her softness, purity, clearness, and sureness; the Spring will remind him of the freshness of their beginning love, the Summer its ripening, and the Autumn of their "golden harvesting"; (to spite Fortune he will not think about Winter at all). Henceforth, Night will be drowned in hope of day. By fighting to preserve health, youth, and beauty they can overcome vicissitudes of fortune.

Declare yourself base fortunes enemy, No less by your contempt than constancy: That I may grow enamoured on your mind, When my own thoughts I there reflected find.

Comment

"Constancy" is an attribute of the heart; by suggesting that "contempt" is an attribute of the mind the speaker proves that there is a way for his love to increase (since he can now love her for qualities of heart and mind). This increase of love, so it is implied, is a victory over Fortune.

He ends with a forthright declaration of his own constancy:

Take therefore all in this: I love so true, As I will never look for less in you.

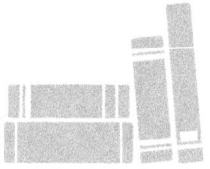

JOHN DONNE

EPICEDES AND OBSEQUIES

Both of the above words refer to what we should describe as "elegies," that is, poems expressing grief at the death of a beloved person. Donne wrote a number of such elegies besides *The First Anniversary*, the finest example of which is his poem on the death of Prince Henry, who died in 1612.

ELEGIE ON THE UNTIMELY DEATH OF THE INCOMPARABLE PRINCE HENRY

The poet begins by asserting that "this Period" (the termination of the Prince's life) is felt by both his centers (of weight and of greatness).

Comment

The technical terminology of "period" and "centers" establishes the basic **metaphor** of the poem; as in the Anniversaries, there are cosmological reverberations flowing from the death of the young prince.

He then explains the literal meaning of the centers; one is of Faith, the other of Reason. All things comprehended in the natural world are the subject of reason, while the "enormous Greatnesses" (such things as God's essence, place, and providence) are the subject of faith. Reason, at its best, almost meets faith, an idea which is illustrated in the young prince:

For, All that Faith could credit mankind could, Reason still seconded that This Prince would.

But both centers are now distracted, and we see not what to believe or to know. Even his reputation acted as a control on neighboring states, and he was his father's greatest instrument for uniting Christianity with the "soul of peace." In the misery of his loss our greatest joy would be to die, just as for earth (the heaviest element) the greatest ambition is "to desire to fall." The only soul which animates us is grief itself.

As with faith, so with reason; reason is the "connection of causes," and as it would be pointless to make inquiries about accidents if all substances were spent, so is it vain to inquire about reason when he (reason's only subject) is gone. Just as when man thinks he discerns the chain of events involved in the pattern of faith, only to be disconcerted by the appearance of some new miracle (a new link in the chain of faith), so now Death having removed the essential link in Reason's chain, it would be pointless for us to try to concoct rational proofs of our own lack of reason. We may "safelier say, that Wee are dead, than hee." The poet closes with a graceful **allusion** to the young woman beloved of the Prince as "that Shee-Intelligence which mov'd This Sphear," and concludes,

I conjure Thee by all the Charmes Hee spoke, By th'Oathes which only you Two never broke, By all the Soules you sigh'd; that if you see These Lines, you wish I knew Your Historie: So, much as You Two mutual Heavens were here, I were an Angel singing what You were.

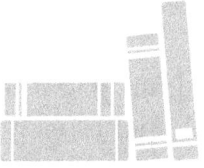

JOHN DONNE

SATYRES

....

Satire is a venerable literary form which treats human institutions with wit, sarcasm, **irony**, and humor, with the object, presumably, of bringing about a reform of those institutions. The models for most later **satire** were the poems of *Juvenal and Persius*, which were rather urbane, general reflections on the follies and foibles of the human race. Donne's *Satyres* deal more specifically with the social types to be met with in late Elizabethan London, and in this sense anticipate (and may even have influenced) the satirical comedies of Jonson and other Jacobean dramatists. The **satires** of Donne were probably all composed early in his career, most likely in the 1590s.

SATYRE III [ON RELIGION]

("Kind pitty chokes my spleene"): The poem takes the form of one half of a conversation - an intemperate invective against the religious vacillation in some unspecified listener. The speaker begins by asserting that it is Religion herself (as opposed to individual sects) who is "worthy of all our Soules devotion." You, who have the means (the "easie wayes" of doctrine and practice) may be damned, and find that pagans of an older day may achieve the end (salvation) simply through strict (ethical) life, which will be accounted equal to faith by God.

Courage, if by that you mean such things as battle, hazardous exploration, or tropical adventures motivated by the hope of gain is mere "courage of straw." Your real foes are the world, the flesh, and the devil. Seek true religion. Where? Mirreus seeks her at Rome, merely because she was there a thousand years ago; Crantz loves only her whom he finds at Geneva - "plaine, simple, sullen, yong." Graius accepts her whom he finds at home here, simply on the persuasions of his guardians. Graccus loves all, on the principle that women, though they may dress differently in different countries, share a single nature.

Comment

Mirreus stands for Roman Catholicism (basing its claim, as Donne sees it, on its ancient lineage); Crantz, presumably, for Calvinism (an extremely ascetic doctrine); Graius for Anglicanism (the "national" religion of an Englishman); Graccus is simply the type of man with no religious persuasion.

You are forced to make a choice, and you seek for truth?

. . . . On a huge hill, Cragged, and steep, Truth stands, and hee that will Reach her, about must, and about must goe.

But make a choice before old age prevents it. Hard deeds pain the body, and hard knowledge pains the mind. Mysteries are like the Sun, dazzling but plain. Let not your Soul be tied to man's law, since it is not by that that it will be tried on the last day:

.... Oh, will it then boot thee To say a Philip, or a Gregory, A Harry or a Martin taught thee this?

Comment

References to Philip of Spain, some Pope Gregory, Henry VIII, and Martin Luther-secular and religious defenders of the faith, two Catholic and two Protestant.

Go back to the primal source of religion. Flowers thrive at the head of the stream, but are destroyed when they are uprooted and carried down by the "streames tyrannous rage."

So perish Soules, which more chuse mens unjust Power from God claym'd, than God himselfe to trust.

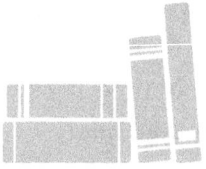

JOHN DONNE

VERSE LETTERS

Verse letters were a common literary form, about which there is little to be said. For the most part they took the form of pretty compliments to friends or patrons, though Donne's were occasionally serious and often managed to be informative.

THE CALME

(This was possibly written in 1597, while Donne was a member of a nautical mission against the Spanish.) The poem is a companion piece to a slightly longer verse letter, *The Storme*, addressed to Donne's friend Christopher Brooke. The title refers to the becalming of the sailing ship on which Donne was berthed; it is one of the more informative epistles, though of course its main purpose was esthetic rather than journalistic. The speaker describes a "stupid calme," which afflicts them even worse than the storm before. The sea is as smooth as a mirror, and the ships as rooted as the isles they sought when they were underway. The pitch is running out of the joints, and the sails are decaying. The seamen's military stations are decorated with rags, the tackle is all "frippery," and in one place lie "feathers and dust."

Comment

There is a kind of irrelevant particularity, a commitment to circumstantial detail, that is typical of a chatty, epistolary style, and that is not found elsewhere in Donne. But this is soon succeeded by a witty interpretation.

Earths hollownesses, which the worlds lungs are, Have no more winde than the upper vault of aire. We can nor lost friends, nor sought foes recover, But meteorlike, save that wee move not, hover.

If, in spite of dangerous fishes, we swim, there is no refreshment in it, and (from the sun) we become "parboyl'd wretches." But the ships continue to languish. Stags, dogs, and all things which move (whether towards, or from) are rewarded with life, or prey, or at least die in action. Fate, however, begrudges all these to us. (But the poem ends with a witty turn,)

Wee have no power, no will, no sense; I lye, I should not then thus feele this miserie.

TO SIR HENRY WOTTON AT HIS GOING AMBASSADOR TO VENICE

In this we have an example of the complimentary verse missive. The poem is in ten **stanzas** of four lines each. It begins with a complimentary definition of an ambassador, couched in references to the part played by various "papers" in the processes of appointment official note taking, and letters of farewell, and asks that this epistle be admitted to their company; it then concludes with an analysis of Sir Henry Wotton's merits as an envoy.

There are three parallel adverbial clauses (**Stanzas** 1 and 2; Stanza 3; and **Stanza** 4) before the main verb, each referring to some kind of "papers" involved in the ambassadorial mission. The first is the royal document of appointment, by which the King transmits his power to Wotton, making him "a Taper of his Torch, a copie writ/ From his Original." The second are the note papers Wotton carries with him, which will guide him in his written communications as well as his official actions. The third are the letters of farewell sent to the ambassador by his friends in their "glad griefe" at his departure. After all these, says the poet, "admit this honest paper," which intends toward Wotton, only what he intends toward the Venetians, that is, a show of love, and a determination to resist all changes that are not characterized by honor.

The poet wants (that is, lacks) the kind of honor Wotton has, but since "'tis an easier load ... to want, than govern greatness,"

'Tis therefore well your spirits now are plac'd In their last Furnace, in activity; Which fits them (Schooles and Courts and Warres o'rpast) To touch and test in any best degree.

Comment

The **metaphor** here is that of alchemy, which uses four concoctions (in four separate furnaces) for the production of the Philosopher's Stone, which has the power to discriminate (by touching) true gold from sophistical gold.

In the last **stanza** the poet promises the ambassador that he will send "oft prayers" to God for his "increase."

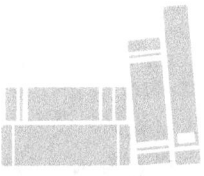

JOHN DONNE

DIVINE POEMS

The difference in subject matter between the *Songs and **Sonnets*** and the *Divine Poems* is sometimes taken, in view of Donne's later career as a clergyman, to support a biographical theory of a young "Jack Donne," a libertine sowing wild oats and recording his excesses in verse, and a chastened John Donne, and Anglican Divine repenting the sins of his youth. The sketchy facts, however, are hardly sufficient to lend substance to this attractive notion. There seems to be a good deal of overlapping in the time covered by the two groups, and it is perhaps best simply to consider the poems on their own merits until the problems of dating have been more adequately treated. *The Divine Poems*, in any case, are characterized by the same sort of witty paradoxes and learned conceits, if not the same subject matter and tone as the *Songs and Sonnets*, though one occasionally finds a jaunty air punctuating the more lugubrious meditations. The following are representative of the full range of matter and technique in the *Divine Poems*.

| GOODFRIDAY, 1613, RIDING WESTWARD:

Since he is riding westward, with his back to Jerusalem (the east), the poet is able to make use not only of the obvious **imagery** of the rising and setting sun, but of the immemorial associations of both these ideas with death and rebirth, and the particularly Christian adaptation of them to the Crucifixion and Resurrection of Christ. He begins with a blunt hypothesis, "Let mans Soule be a Spheare," and proceeds to work out the analogies between celestial mechanics and social obligations. Pleasure and business are the soul's primum mobile, forcibly moving it toward the west when its own inclination ("naturall forme") should move it toward the east. There it should see a "Sunne" (note the sun/son pun) setting, but thereby begetting endless day. But, the poet admits, he almost dares to be glad that he does not have to gaze on a spectacle which made even Nature shrink, and made His "footstoole crack" (the earthquake) and "the Sunne winke" (the eclipse). How could be behold the hands which span the poles pierced with nails, or the blood "which is the seat of all our Souls . . . made durt of dust."

Comment

This image is an excellent illustration of Donne's peculiar blending of stark **realism** with "**metaphysical**" conceit. The pathos of Good Friday comes through admirably, and one feels the speaker's genuine sense of Christ's love for mankind as proved by the bleeding wounds. This is mingled, however, with the bizarre observation that Christ's blood (part of His mortal, human body) falls in droplets to the ground, where it mingles with the soil and becomes "durt."

He thinks, as he continues westward, that he is turning his back on Christ, but solaces himself with the consideration that this is merely to receive "corrections, till thy mercies bid thee leave." He asks to have his rusts and deformities burned off.

Restore thine Image, so much, by thy grace, That thou may'st know mee, and I'll turne my face.

Comment

The poem displays a fine handling of tone, **imagery**, and structure. The opening lines, with their imperative mood and intellectual timbre, suggest a tight rational control. But as the image of Christ becomes more vivid it is as if the speaker were forced to abandon his willful rhetoric and to adopt a more humble attitude. The man who says, in a simple, colloquial tone, "That thou may'st know mee, and I'll turne my face," is a man who has been affected by the experience with which the poem deals.

HOLY SONNETS

These nineteen **sonnets** were not all written after Donne's ordination, or after the death of his wife (in 1617), an opinion once widely entertained. Their tone, however, is for the most part extraordinarily personal. The accustomed wit is there, but subdued to a keen sense of emotional urgency.

Holy Sonnet I

The speaker asks God, Who has made him, whether He will let His work decay. He runs toward death, pleasures pall, the eyes are dimming, despair dogs his tracks, and death looms ahead. The "old subtle foe" tempts him, but

Thy Grace may wing me to prevent his art, And thou like Adamant draw mine iron heart.

Holy Sonnet V

This begins with the famous lines (a religious application of the macrocosm/microcosm figure),

I am a little world made cunningly Of Elements and an Angelike spright But black sinne hath betraid to endlesse night My worlds both parts, and (oh) both parts must die.

He implores the astronomers (discoverers of new worlds) to pour new seas into his eyes so that he might drown his world (an **allusion** to the Deluge), or at least wash it (in tears of repentance). "But oh it must be burnt!" Since lust and envy have burned it before, let them give way to the fire of zeal, "which doth in eating heale."

Holy Sonnet VII

The octave of the **sonnet** is a command to the summoning angels to blow their trumpets "at the round earth's imagined corners;" this is followed by a catalogue of all mankind dividend according to the multifarious ways in which they have met death, and a command to obey the summons. The list includes:

All whom warre, dearth, age, agues, tyrannies, Despaire, law, chance, hath slaine, and you whose eyes Shall behold God, and never tast deaths woe. [The last people on earth at the moment of the call to the General Judgment].

The sestet abruptly changes the mood of these grandiose imperatives, and humbly asks God to give the speaker time to mourn for his sins, ending:

Teach mee how to repent; for that's as good As if thou'hadst seal'd my pardon, with thy blood.

Comment

The efficacy of the Redemption (Christ's blood) is dependent upon the individual sinner's contrition for his sins. What the last lines mean is that repentance, in the speaker's case, is as sure a guarantee of absolution as if he carried a written pardon, sealed (as any document is sealed with wax) with the blood of Christ. What is noteworthy about the closing **couplet** is the blunt, colloquial tone, with its implication of close familiarity.

Holy Sonnet IX

This **sonnet** opens with an oft-quoted quatrain:

If poysonous mineralls, and if that tree, Whose fruit threw death on else immortall us, If lecherous goats, if serpents envious Cannot be damn'd; Alas; why should I bee?

Comment

Here we note the "chain of being" in reverse order: minerals, vegetable (that tree), animal (goats and serpents), and man

(I, the speaker), each particular item being the poisonous or baleful member of its species. Sin is of course only possible to a rational creature, but Donne insinuates that there is an inequity involved in this.

The querulous tone of the octave, however, is followed by one of resignation and humility in the sestet, as the speaker asks for nothing more than to be forgotten by God.

Holy Sonnet X

This famous **sonnet**, "Death be not proud, though some have called thee / Mighty and dreadful," is a skillful and imaginative piece of sophistry designed to prove that death has no power over the Christian soul. Sleep, death's "picture," causes pleasure; the best men embrace death the soonest; death is merely the tool of Fate, Chance, kings, and desperadoes, and finally (a triumphant assertion of Christian belief in an afterlife),

One short sleepe past, wee wake eternally, And death shall be no more; death, thou shalt die.

Holy Sonnet XIV

The speaker demands that the "three-person'd God" batter his heart, "breake, blowe, burn" and make him new (as a blacksmith would with a damaged vessel), and not merely to "knocke, breathe, shine, and seeke to mend" (as one might work on a merely dented object).

Comment

The blacksmith image is intricately connected with the reference to the Trinity, since both "break" and "knock" suggest the figure of God the Father, "blow" and "breathe" the Holy Spirit (in Latin, spiritus = breath), while "burn" and "shine" are probably intended to refer to Christ (perhaps on the basis on Donne's not infrequent son/sun pun, though even this may be connected with iconographical associations between Christ and Apollo, the sun god).

The second quatrain visualizes the sinner as a usurped town, betrayed by a weak Reason; the third pictures him as a woman betrothed to her enemy. The main idea, namely that in every case violent means must be resorted to, gains paradoxical expression in the final four lines:

Divorce mee, `untie, or breake that knot againe, Take mee to you, imprison mee, for I Except you'enthrall mee, never shall be free, Nor ever chast, except you ravish mee.

A HYMNE TO GOD THE FATHER

This poem in three **stanzas** is an abject plea for forgiveness, the sincerity of which should probably not be questioned, though for a modern reader the continual play upon his own name may seem a bit ostentatious.

When thou hast done, thou hast not done [Donne] For, I have more.

The last **stanza** also makes use of the pun on `sun' and `son': "Thy sonne / Shall shine as he shines now."

HYMNE TO GOD MY GOD, IN MY SICKNESSE

This poem is richer in **imagery** than the preceding, and the punning, by being worked into the **theme** more imaginatively, does not stand out so strongly. The speaker first sees himself (in Platonic terms) as one about to be made a part of the celestial harmonies, and thus having to "tune the instrument" before he enters the room. Flat on his back in his sickness, he sees himself (in a new version of the macrocosm/microcosm conceit) as a "flatt Map" (a Mercator projection), in which West and East, while they seem to be different are actually one, and so "death doth touch the Resurrection." He wonders about his destination; will it be the "Pacifique Sea"? (with a pun on Latin pax, pacis, peace), the "Easterne riches"? or Jerusalem? (Each of these may be taken as an aspect of the rewards of Heaven.) But the only way to any of these is through "streights" (a pun on geographical "straits" and the same word in its wider meaning, as "in straitened circumstances"). The poet next alludes to the common medieval notion that the infamous tree of Eden yielded the wood for Christ's cross (as aspect of the general interpretation of Christ as the "second Adam"), and asserts that both Adams may be seen in him:

As the first Adams sweat surrounds my face, May the last Adams blood my soule embrace.

He begs that, wrapped in Christ's purple (that is, his blood), he may be received into Heaven; that by wearing these thorns (the pains of the disease) he may gain the other crown (of glory); and as he preached the word of God to others, he may himself become an illustration of the text, "Therefore that he may raise the Lord throws down."

SUMMARY

The Divine Poems display a fervor, a genuine faith, and a convincing humility despite the occasional excesses of wit. It should be noted that even in his sermons (and these far outweigh the poems in bulk) Donne continually wrests remote meanings from words and images in the tradition of medieval Biblical exegesis, practiced by men for whom the entire world was an intricate system of analogous phenomena. "Wit," in this sense, was an intellectual habit to which Donne had been conditioned by his intense reading in medieval sermons and theological works, as well as by his training in rhetoric. As for the *Holy* **Sonnets** in particular, they illustrate an impressive mastery of the **sonnet** form, but demonstrate also that Donne could adapt it to his purposes and depart from the strict octave-sestet form (or the English form) when the emotional stress of the poem demanded a less rigorous structure.

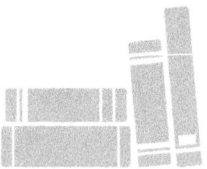

GEORGE HERBERT

INTRODUCTION

Herbert was born in 1593, the son of Magdalen Herbert, to whom a number of Donne's poems were addressed and of Richard Herbert. He attended Westminster School, and went on to Trinity College, Cambridge, of which he became a fellow and later a Reader in Rhetoric, and where he undertook theological studies which led to his ordination in 1630 as an Anglican priest, and his appointment to the parish of Bemerton, near Salisbury. Only after his death in 1633 did Herbert's English poems appear in print. His chief work, a collection of religious lyrics, is entitled *The Temple*.

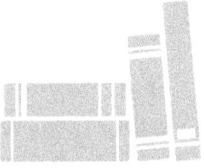

THE METAPHYSICAL POETS

THE COLLAR

The titles of Herbert's poems frequently suggest a basic metaphorical structure, which is not again alluded to specifically in the poem. This clearly shows the influence of the Emblem Books, which contained pictorial symbols on religious themes, with prose explications of their esoteric meanings.

Comment

The "collar" of the poem is first of all a metonymic reference to the priesthood itself, not merely because a clerical collar is a priest's distinguishing mark, but because it implies the entire set of restraints which characterize the life of a priest. This derives from the secondary meaning of "collar" as an iron ring with which serfs had at one time been bound. The basic motion of the poem is away from a narrowing conception of the religious life deriving from spiritual aridity towards a free acceptance of the Divine Lordship.

The speaker begins with an outburst complaining of the fact that though free by nature and lineage he must still be "in suit" (begging for some favor, though perhaps with a pun on "suit" as clerical garb). Where before there was wine and corn (a possible reference to the sacrament of the Eucharist) now there is only a harvest of thorns. Are the years flowers all blasted? All wasted?

It is clear that it is the heart that has been complaining, and now another side of the speaker's personality (possibly the mind) rebukes it. "Leave thy cold dispute," the heart is told, "forsake thy cage, thy rope of sands," which has become a law to you. You are being controlled by a "death's head," by fear itself.

He that forbears To suit and serve his need, Deserves his load. But as I rav'd and grew more fierce and wilde At every word, Me thoughts I heard one calling, Childe! And I reply'd, My Lord.

Comment

The altered meaning of "suit" (now signifying adaptation or adjustment) suggests the point of view of the rational mind, and seems to point to a conclusion in which head conquers heart. But, under the influence of the heart, he grows "more fierce and wilde," until the Father's call elicits his humble submission. This reliance on simple faith to quell doubts and emotional turbulence is typical of Herbert's poetry.

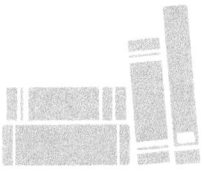

GEORGE HERBERT

THE PULLEY

....

(Next to *The Collar* this is perhaps Herbert's most often read lyric.) The title suggests that in the Divine economy, the method by which souls are conveyed upward to Heaven may be looked at under the metaphor of a mechanical contrivance. At the creation, God bestowed strength, beauty, wisdom, honor, and pleasure on man, but when the only gift remaining to be dealt out was "rest," God halted. If this were to be given to man, he would adore "my gifts instead of me,/ And rest in Nature, not the God of Nature."

Yet let him keep the rest, But keep them with repining restlessnesse; Let him be rich and wearie, that at least, If goodnesse leade him not, yet wearinesse May tosse him to my breast.

Comment

The punning on "rest" ("remainder" and "repose") is handled with such open-hearted simplicity that it is hard to think of Herbert as being "witty" in the taut, intellectual manner of

Donne. Even the **metaphor** of the pulley conveys a sharp sense of elementary (almost childlike) emotional response to the mystery of God's ways.

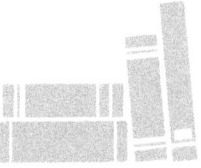

GEORGE HERBERT

THE ALTAR

The Altar is an example of patterned verse, in which the lines are so composed, and the poem so arranged, typographically, that it makes up a picture, or at least an outline, of the very thing which is the subject of the poem. Of this poem's sixteen lines, lines 1, 2, 15, and 16 are pentameter; lines 3, 4, 13, and 14 are **tetrameter** and lines 5 through 12 are **dimeter**. The whole is arranged symmetrically, with the top and bottom flaring out like the table top and base of an altar. Furthermore, lines 5 and 6: "A Heart alone / Is such a stone," introduce the "heart" of the poem/altar. This sort of affectation must be regarded as little more than an extreme curiosity, though it had a strange hold over Herbert, and he alone among the chief metaphysical poets practiced it to any extraordinary degree, though he achieved some remarkable results.

REDEMPTION

This is one of Herbert's more interesting shorter lyrics, showing the sort of simple grasp of cosmic interrelationships that the medieval mind often displayed. The opening lines introduce the speaker as a tenant seeking a lord, so that he might substitute a "new small-rented lease" for an old. At his manor in heaven he is told that the lord has gone to earth to take possession of some "dearly bought" land. Searching for him in vain in all the great resorts, the speaker at length hears

.... a ragged noise and mirth Of theeves and murderers: there I him espied, Who straight, Your suit is granted, said, & died.

Comment

Herbert here shows an astonishing power of compression without a loss of essential meaning. And there is nothing overly subtle about the poem, nor is surprise the chief effect aimed at (the Lord/lord analogy is clear from the beginning). But there is a delicate art of allusive understatement at work in a way that is hard to define.

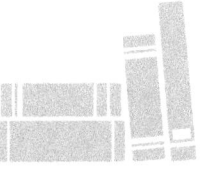

GEORGE HERBERT

EASTER-WINGS

This is another pattern poem, and was originally printed sideways on facing pages so that its two **stanzas** resembled a pair of wings. Following is the first half of the first stanza:

Lord, who createdst man in wealth and store, Though foolishly he lost the same, Decaying more and more, Till he became Most poore:

COMMENT

The form illustrates (what the poem states) decay and gradual diminution of man's primal virtues and powers.

    The second half of the **stanza** then expands, corresponding to the idea it expresses, namely, that the speaker wishes to "rise" (as Christ rose on Easter Sunday) towards Heaven. The second **stanza** is identical in structure, moving from a statement about the poet's "tender age" to the time when, through God's chastising hand, he became "most thinne"; it then expands towards the conclusion (analogous to the fact that the Crucifixion was the necessary prerequisite to the Resurrection) that "Affliction shall advance the flight in me."

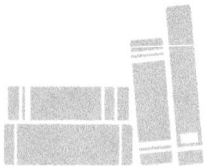

GEORGE HERBERT

JORDAN

The poet here speaks of the relationship of rhetorical devices to the expression of religious devotion. At first, he says, he sought out "quaint words" and "trim inventions," "curling with **metaphors** a plain intention." Fanciful notions sprang up in his head by the thousands, and he often blotted what he first wrote, something seeming too dead, other too plain.

Nothing could seem too rich to clothe the sunne, Much lesse those joyes which trample on his head.

As he bustled to weave himself into the sense of his lines, he heard a friend whisper: "There is in love a sweetnesse readie penn'd: / Copie out onely that, and save expense" (that is, "Be yourself, and write what is in your heart.").

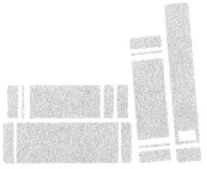

ABRAHAM COWLEY

INTRODUCTION

Cowley was born in 1618, attended Westminster School and later Trinity College, Cambridge. During the civil war and in the early years of the Commonwealth he carried on activities for the Royalist party, taking up residence at Oxford in 1643, and then going on to France, where he became secretary to Lord Jermyn. He was imprisoned upon his return to London, though shortly released, whereupon he took up the study of medicine. (Johnson, in his *Life of Cowley*, suggests that the extent of his cooperation with the men in power is hard to assess, and that Cowley perhaps should not be blamed for his compliance.) He was interested in science, and had, in fact, been proposed for membership in the Royal Society. His *Poems* were published in 1656. Cowley is probably best remembered for his Pindaric odes.

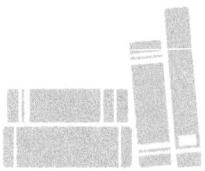

ABRAHAM COWLEY

TO THE ROYAL SOCIETY

Cowley's famous ode "To the Royal Society" was written in 1667 to be prefixed to Sprat's *History of the Royal Society*. [**Stanza 1**]: Philosophy, the poet declares, has been kept in bondage for three or four thousand years, in which time it might well have been brought to perfection had not its guardians suppressed its "natural powers" lest it put an end to their "authority." [**Stanza 2**]: They amused him (that is, Philosophy) with "wanton wit," poetic fancies, and tortuous speculations, instead of carrying him to see "Nature's endless Treasurie," until,

Bacon at last, a mighty Man arose Whom a wise King and Nature chose Lord Chancellour of both their Lawes, And boldly undertook the injur'd Pupils cause.

Comment

Francis Bacon, who was Lord Chancellor of England under James I, wrote his Novum Organum in an effort to free human thought from what he regarded as the shackles of Aristotelian philosophy (particularly vicious, as he thought, in its substitution of speculative ideas for observed scientific fact) and Scholastic argument (the discussions of the medieval Schoolmen, philosophers most of whose endeavors struck Bacon as useless hairsplitting).

[**Stanza** 3]: With "the plain magick of true Reason's light" Bacon vanquished "authority" (ancient authors like Aristotle were continually appealed to as "authorities" whose opinions were incontrovertible). He broke the "scare-crow Deity" which ruled men's minds and substituted reliance on sense experience for pure mental gymnastics,

For 'tis God only who can find All Nature in his mind.

[**Stanza** 4]: He made things rather than words the "Mind's right Object," extracting from real rather than painted grapes a "refreshing wine" for men's souls. [**Stanza** 5]: Like Moses leading the Hebrews out of captivity, Bacon led men to the borders of the promised land of scientific discovery. It is no wonder that he was able only to point the way, and not to "fadome the vast depths of Nature's Sea," since he was always either in the depths of affliction or on the heights of triumph, and time was not allotted to him. [**Stanza** 6]: Cowley next addresses the "great Champions" (that is, the members of the Royal Society), who will go out to subdue the armies of entrenched learning just like Gideon's little band. [**Stanza** 7]: The lights of victory can already be described in the "new scenes of heaven" and "crowds of golden Worlds on high" and they have even.

... taught the curious Sight to press Into the privatest recess Of her imperceptible littleness.

Comment

These are of course references to the recent great astronomical discoveries, particularly such things as Kepler's observations of comets and novae, and Galileo's discovery of the moons of Jupiter and of a multitude of previously unobserved stars, as well as to Hooke's *Micrographia*, the record of the examinations of the microscopical world made with that new instrument.

[**Stanza** 8]: Cowley next calls down a curse on those who seek to ridicule or scorn these maiden scientific efforts, so noble in design, so human in their utility, so divine in the way they extend man's knowledge. Ignorance and envious wit have ever been the lot of those who do battle against entrenched intellectual phantoms. [**Stanza** 9]: Bidding the members "courage and success," Cowley congratulates them on having chosen such a worthy historian, who has "vindicated Eloquence and Wit" in a "candid style" which has a "comely Dress without the paint of Art."

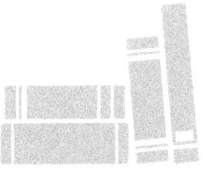

ABRAHAM COWLEY

ODE: OF WIT

The poet, addressing himself to some unidentified "thou" (though it is possibly Thomas Sprat) asks what sort of thing Wit is, since it bears a "thousand different shapes," and deceives men as to its real nature. It is common for a man to be called a "wit," yet it is usually merely for jests and "florid talk," Wit is not the forcing of lifeless verses, or the adorning and gilding of parts or a profusion of details. It is not merely verbal punning (little better than anagrams and acrostics), nor is it to be found in unseemly double-entendres. It is not to be seen in mere empty ranting, nor in "a tall **Metaphor** in the Bombast way," nor in epigrammatic statements. Can it only be defined by negatives, he asks, and replies to this question with the eighth stanza:

In a true piece of Wit all things must be, Yet all things there agree. As in the Ark, joyn'd without force or strife, All Creatures dwelt; all Creatures that had Life. Or as the Primitive Forms of all (If we compare great things with small) Which without Discord or Confusion lie, In that strange Mirror of the Deitie.

Comment

The analogy between the poet and the Creator is of course an ancient idea, which had been taken with renewed seriousness on many previous occasions. What is interesting here, is that Cowley enlists it in the service of wit, a concept that occupied many of the century's best minds.

The last **stanza** compliments the person addressed in the Ode, by declaring that when asked

What thing right Wit, and height of Genius is, I'll onely shew your Lines, and say, 'Tis This.

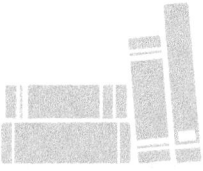

ABRAHAM COWLEY

THE WISH

....

(This poem may serve as an example of Cowley's light, amatory verse in the **metaphysical** style borrowed from Donne. These lyrics are collected in his work entitled *The Mistress*.) The poet pities those caught up in the busy concourse of the world, those who must endure the "crowd, and buzz, and murmurings / Of this great hive, the city." He wishes for himself merely a house and garden, a few friends and many books, and, since "love ne'er will from me flee,"

A mistress moderately fair, And good as guardian angels are, Only beloved, and loving me!

He apostrophizes the fountains, fields, and woods, and wonders when he will be their "happy tenant." Pride and ambition appear in this rustic setting "only in far-fetched metaphors." He could live happy here with "one dear she" who is all the world and could even "exclude / In deserts, solitude."

I should have then this only fear, Lest men, when they my pleasures see, Should hither throng to live like me, And so make a city here.

COMMENT

This is typical enough of the verses in *The Mistress*. While they are in the **metaphysical** style, in the sense that they employ unusual **metaphors** and learned scientific notions, for the most part they lack Donne's imaginative pressure and his sense of sincerity.

HENRY VAUGHAN

INTRODUCTION

Henry Vaughan, the Silurist (so-called after the section of Wales from which he came), was educated at Oxford, probably at Jesus College. He saw service in the Royalist cause, later studied medicine and became a practicing doctor. His *Olor Iscanus* (1651), consisted mostly of translations, but *Silex Scintillans* (1655), showed the clear influence of Herbert's *The Temple* even while it struck a new note of mysticism and Platonic interest in nature. There is a "romantic" strain in Vaughan, which seems to anticipate the poetry of Wordsworth, though it is fairly certain that Wordsworth and the other Romantics were not familiar with his verse.

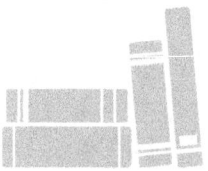

HENRY VAUGHAN

THE WORLD

In four fifteen-line **stanzas** Vaughan opposes to his mystical vision of eternity as "a great ring of pure and endless light" a catalogue of all the vicious, vain, and fatuous types to be found in the world below. There is the doting lover, with all the accoutrements of the wooing game, "wit's sour delights"; the darksome statesman, with "condemning thoughts, like mad eclipses," scowling at his soul; the "fearful miser on a heap of rust," hardly trusting his own hands; the "downright epicure," whose heaven is sense; and all the weaker sort, who are enslaved by trivialities. Poor, despised Truth sat by, noting the victory of these things over men.

Yet some, who all this while did weep and sing, And sing and weep, soared up into the ring; But most would use no wing.

Comment

These are apparently the meaner sort of religious sectaries, who, by a mis-directed kind of enthusiasm and asceticism, hope to merit heaven. The "wing" must refer to a kind of mystical union, not dependent on sense and the weaker sort of emotions.

But as he discussed their folly, one whispered to another: "This ring the Bridegroom did for none provide, / But for His bride."

Comment

This quotation from Revelation 21:9 is usually taken to refer to Christ (the Heavenly Bridegroom) and the Christian soul (the bride). There is something enigmatic about the way Vaughan employs it, however, and we are made to wonder whether it is finally a criticism of their madness or his mystical isolation.

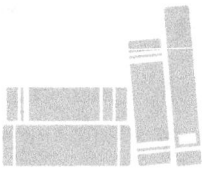

HENRY VAUGHAN

THE RETREAT

(This poem is based on the Platonic notion of the soul's pre-existence. Being born is the process of taking on the inhibiting freight of the fleshly body; it merely obscures the celestial vision which the child carries with him into the world.) The poet looks back to those early days when he shone in his "angel infancy," a time before his understanding (as opposed to the imagination) had begun to interfere with his soul's "white, celestial thought." As a child, he perceived in the "weaker glories" of nature (such things as clouds and flowers) "some shadows of eternity" (a phrase bearing a curious resemblance to Wordsworth's Intimations of Immortality). Before he learned the "black art" of sin, he

. . . felt through all this fleshly dress Bright shoots of everlastingness.

The second verse paragraph expresses the hope that he might again return to the heavenly city, a journey which is being prevented by a soul which "is drunk, and staggers in the way."

Some men a forward motion love; But I by backward steps would move, And when this dust falls to the urn, In that state I came, return.

> Comment

This poem might well be used as a discriminant for the concepts "childish" and "childlike." Beneath the superficial simplicity there is a sense of masterful control and a genius for the significant phrase ("angel infancy," "gilded cloud," "weaker glories," or "bright shoots of everlastingness"). Vaughan has the power to suggest the luminous world of the young child, without descending to childish concepts.

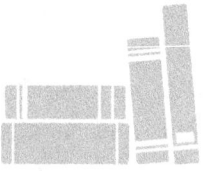

THE METAPHYSICAL POETS

CRITICAL COMMENTARY

EIGHTEENTH AND NINETEENTH CENTURIES

Formal criticism of the **metaphysical** poets may be said to begin with Samuel Johnson, and his famous condemnation contained in the *Life of Cowley* (1779):

> Wit, like all other things subject by their nature to the choice of man, has its changes and fashions, and a different times takes different forms. About the beginning of the seventeenth century, appeared a race of writers that may be termed the **metaphysical** poets; of whom, in a criticism on the works of Cowley, it is not improper to give some account.
>
> The **metaphysical** poets were men of learning, and to show their learning was their whole endeavour: but, unluckily resolving to show it in rhyme, instead of writing poetry they only wrote verses, and very often such verse as stood the trial of the finger better than of the ear . . .
>
> . . . Their thoughts are often new, but seldom natural; they are not obvious, but neither are they just; and the reader, far

from wondering that he missed them, wonders more frequently by what perverseness of industry they were ever found.

... The most heterogeneous ideas are yoked by violence together; nature and art are ransacked for illustrations, comparisons, and allusions; their learning instructs, and their subtilty surprises; but the reader commonly thinks his improvement dearly bought, and though he sometimes admires, is seldom pleased.

Johnson's blast is a magnificent and entertaining piece of rhetoric, but precisely what we would expect the neo-Classical attitude to be. With rare exceptions, the opinion of the Romantics was equally unfavorable. An anonymous critic, writing in 1823, could, while admitting the general charge of obscurity and harshness, find many instances of "clear and smooth construction" and a "passionate sweetness and softness" of verse; and, while conceding that almost every beauty was accompanied by a "striking deformity" irritating in the extreme, was able to claim that the poetry was redeemed by "an unceasing activity and an over-flowing fullness of mind." Even De Quincey condemned Johnson's opinion, and was willing to grant the excellence of Donne's poetry "tried by its own laws" - which are the laws of rhetoric rather than of poetry. Coleridge saw Donne as a poet "whose muse on dromedary trots," and, despite occasional fervency and tenderness, as a mere practitioner of wit. Interest in the **metaphysicals** was a thin trickle throughout the latter half of the nineteenth century, and Saintsbury's bafflingly ambiguous appraisal (1896) fittingly closes the period. At one point he speaks of Donne's "frequent involution and eccentricity, his ... indulgence in extravagances which go near to silliness, [causing the reader to] lose the extraordinary beauties which lie beyond or among those faults." At another, he proposes Donne as the perfect poet for a man who understands "the alternations not merely of passion and satiety, but of passion and laughter, of melancholy reflection, or passion earthly enough and spiritual rapture almost heavenly."

THE TWENTIETH CENTURY

The **metaphysical** revival of our time dates from Sir H. J. C. Grierson's edition of *The Poems of John Donne* in 1912. In addition to the very great merit of having provided the first scholarly edition of Donne, Grierson offered a balanced critical appraisal of the poet, noting that his "wit [is touched] with fancy, his reflections with imagination, his vision with passion." It was only the force of Donne's personality, he suggested, "that could achieve even an approximate harmony of elements so divergent as are united in his love-verses, that could master the lower-natured steed that drew the chariot of his troubled and passionate soul ..." And in his *Holy Sonnets*, Professor Grierson found "an intensely human note." The Donne edition was followed (in 1921) by Grierson's anthology, **Metaphysical** *Lyrics and Poems of the Seventeenth Century*, a book which impressed Eliot and elicited his famous essay on *The* **Metaphysical** *Poets* (1921). It was here that Eliot spoke of the metaphysicals' "direct sensuous apprehension of thought, or a re-creation of thought into feeling," and mildly rebuked the poets of the nineteenth century, who, unlike Donne, did "not feel their thought as immediately as the odour of a rose. A thought to Donne was an experience; it modified his sensibility." Eliot also placed these poets "in the direct current of English poetry" and, by his own adaptation of the **metaphysical** style, was probably the chief cause of their popularity for the next forty years.

Pierre Legouis set out (in 1928) to exonerate Donne from the charge of being a romantic sensualist, and ended by explaining all of Donne's lyric verse in terms of a highly rarefied technique and an impersonal art. Typical of Legouis' approach is his analysis of the ending of *Loves Deitie:* "The poet knows he must end on a statement similar in form, though directly opposite in meaning to the concluding statements of the preceding **stanza**, and I chiefly admire the cleverness with which he manages to fit all the logical joints into the last three lines." M. Legouis was of the opinion that Donne's life may have been wild, "but when he set to indite a love-poem, or vent in verse a theory on problems of sexual morality, he composed himself and looked about for literary devices to improve his theme." One of the earliest of the "new critical" voices was that of Empson (in *Seven Types of Ambiguity*, 1930), whose brilliant but sometimes eccentric interpretations were probably more convincing in the case of Donne and his followers than in the case of Keats or Wordsworth. At his best, as when demonstrating just how Crashaw's **metaphors** (in the *Hymne ... to St. Teresa*) convey "a strange mixture of feeling," Empson is very effective, as is his analysis of Donne's *A Valediction: Of Weeping"* (pp. 158 - 168 in the Vintage Edition). Close textual analysis, with the main emphasis on ambiguity, **irony**, and paradox, is also the approach taken by Cleanth Brooks in his essay on *Donne's The Canonization* (Chapter 1 of his influential work, *The Well Wrought Urn*). Empson's and Brooks' theoretical positions may be traced to the influence of Eliot and of I. A. Richards, whose *Principles of Literary Criticism* (1925) and *Practical Criticism* (1929) encouraged the "close reading" of texts and found very congenial subject matter in **metaphysical** poetry.

A return to a more conventional historical approach (which at the same time assimilates the techniques of careful verbal and metrical analysis) may be noted in Joan Bennett's *Four Metaphysical Poets* (1934). Miss Bennett's book was especially useful for her close scrutiny of the debt the later poets owed to Donne. Her analysis of *Herbert's Love* (III) shows a sensitive appreciation of the way in which Herbert, unlike Donne, "develops his single situation at leisure and governs his reader's emotion almost entirely by his management of the tension." The equally sensitive, but far more elaborate study by Helen C. White (1936), which ranges through the literary, religious, and cultural background of the poetry, clearly establishes the fact that metaphysical poetry was no "sport of nature" but had deep roots in the emotional and intellectual climate of the day. What Miss White's book accomplished for the relationship of religious traditions to the poetry, Charles M. Coffin's *John Donne and the New Philosophy* (1937) did for the scientific currents of the day. Coffin's book is a perceptive analysis of the part played in Donne's **imagery** by such works as Gilbert's *On the Magnet* and Kepler's *De Stella Nova*. Complementing these earlier studies by confining itself more exclusively to literary traditions and to the change of literary sensibility in the course of the seventeenth century is R. L. Sharp's *From Donne to Dryden* (1940). Sharp's description of the change relies heavily on his analysis of the controversy between Hobbes and Davenant, centering on the nature of literary expression and its relation to such concepts as wit, fancy, and imagination. Treating Donne from a more philosophical point of view is M. F. Moloney's book, *John Donne: His Flight From Medievalism* (1944), which sees the tension in Donne's poetry a result of his being torn between the claims of medieval supernaturalism and the newly revived pagan naturalism. Though written as a contribution to the *Oxford History of English Literature* (Vol. V - 1945) and therefore not intended to espouse any one critical position, Douglas Bush's humane and incisive essay on "Johnson, Donne, and their Successors" (Chapter IV) is indispensable reading. By 1945, at least, the fast multiplying array of books and articles on **metaphysical** poetry (mainly, thus far, on Donne) was witness to the silent revolution in taste which had occurred.

A growing interest on the part of literary critics in the "history of ideas," particularly the influence of scientific invention and discovery on the literary imagination, found its application to the **metaphysicals** in Marjorie Nicolson's now famous book, *The Breaking of the Circle* (1949). Professor Nicolson's work traces the workings of the medieval world picture in the poetry of the early part of the century, and analyzes the fragmentation wrought in the sensibility of later poets by the new cosmology and physiology. Joseph Mazzeo, developing similar interests, has published a number of articles in the past decade devoted to the influence of the world picture on seventeenth-century poetry (for example, "Notes on John Donne's Alchemical Imagery," included in his *Renaissance and Seventeenth-Century Studies*). During the same period the outstanding scholarly and textual work on Donne's poetry (accompanied by sane and gracious critical remarks) has been carried out by Helen Gardner in her *The Divine Poems of John Donne* (Oxford, 1952), and, most recently, *The Love Poems of John Donne* (Oxford, 1965).

Of the more exclusively critical appraisals of Donne in recent years, J. B. Leishman's *The Monarch of Wit* is noteworthy, having gone through six editions between 1951 and 1962. Leishman follows a moderate biographical approach, with a heavy emphasis on Donne's debt to classical forerunners. A good deal of the impudent wit we note in Donne's *Elegies*, for example, is traced by Leishman to specific sources in Ovid's *Amores*. A number of books, such as Clay Hunt's *Donne's Poetry* (1954) and Doniphan Louthan's *The Poetry of John Donne* (1951) confine themselves to the exhaustive explication of specific poems. Of books of this sort, which adopt a more eclectic approach to the matter of sources and influences, and which rely heavily on taste and ingenuity, Arnold Stein's *John Donne's Lyrics: The Eloquence of Action* is a reasonable and sensitive approach to the problem of a modern reader's response.

Book-length studies of the other **metaphysical** poets have been sparser. We may note R. B. Hinman's *Abraham Cowley's World of Order* (1960), Austin Warren's *Richard Crashaw* (1939), Joseph Summers' *George Herbert* (1954) as being among the more important. Otherwise, study of the minor poets has been carried on in the critical and scholarly journals. The tide of critical curiosity seemed most full in the early 'fifties, and there seems to be a general slackening of interest in the present decade. But there is no question of the fact that **metaphysical** poetry (especially Donne) has been firmly established in the canon of respectable and important English literature.

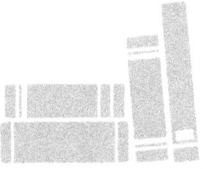

THE METAPHYSICAL POETS

ESSAY QUESTIONS AND ANSWERS

Question: Compare Marvell's treatment of the macrocosm/microcosm figure with Donne's, as seen in their short lyrics.

Answer: Marvell's *On a Drop of Dew* and Donne's *A Valediction: Of Weeping* are typical of their authors and form an apt basis of comparison. In one a dew drop, in the other a tear, is made metaphorically a world. Donne's tears, catching his mistress' image as they fall, are thus made globes, even worlds, until their tears jointly flood the very world they stand on, a flood which represents the dissolution of his heaven (particularly, the watery firmament). The whole conceit is carefully controlled, semi-playful, and all in the service of defining a personal relationship and the emotions which circumstances evoke from it. Marvell is as precise as Donne. His drop of dew, for instance, "frames as it can its native element" (that is, within its own limited scope, reproduces the elemental watery sphere of Aristotelian cosmology), and he notes that the sun evaporates the dew drop ("exhales it back again"). But in Marvell there is a keener interest in nature for its own sake, an interest touched by philosophical considerations. He is concerned with the details of a cosmological system in which dew drops can be charged with a sacramental significance and be symbolic of human souls. It is not that Marvell is a better or worse poet than Donne, but that their interests are dissimilar. Donne's, at least in his lyrics, are extremely personal; Marvell seems constantly probing for philosophical and mystical insight

Question: Illustrate and explain the use of "organic **metaphor**" by the **metaphysical** poets.

Answer: The **metaphysical** poets, particularly in the early years of their "rediscovery," were highly praised for their use of organic **metaphors** as opposed to the (as it was once, but no longer widely thought) "decorative" **metaphors** of the Augustan poets. In "new critical" terms, a poem has both texture (rhythm, **imagery** etc.) and structure (controlling **theme**, relationship of parts), and these in a successful poem can be logically but not really separated. A **metaphor** is organic when the texture and structure are successfully blended, when the **metaphor** is so integrally a part of the poem that its removal would be tantamount to doing away with the poem. Any of Herbert's "emblematic" poems, *The Collar*, for example, illustrates this instantly, as compared, let us say, with Cowley's *The Thief*. The third stanza of *The Thief* could be omitted without any loss to the sense of the poem, while, on the contrary, every image in *The Collar* contributes essentially to the central conception. Donne's *Lovers Infiniteness* is a particularly apt illustration of this idea, since it is built around the double conception of lovers as representing in their own way the scholastic doctrine of infinity, and of lovers as involved in an economic relationship based on the necessity of getting a quid pro quo. It is absolutely impossible to detach either of these conceptions from the poem, and be left with the same poem. The terminology of "treasure," "bargain," gave, all, stocks, rewards, loss, save etc. grows naturally out of the economic **metaphor**, while that of infinite, all, partial, growth etc. stems from the "infinity" idea. In this poem, furthermore, the two terminologies overlap, making it even more difficult to conceive of their detachment from the poem. At root, of course, the idea of an "organic **metaphor**" is not vastly different from the commonsense notion of consistency and relationship of parts; as first applied to Donne, it was probably an attempt to generate respect for **metaphysical** poetry by showing that it fulfilled preeminently Coleridge's strictures concerning organic form.

Question: How does Herbert's handling of a religious **theme** compare with Donne's?

Answer: For this purpose, Donne's *Holy **Sonnet** XVI* ("Batter my heart, three-person'd God") and Herbert's *Repentance* serve admirably. Donne's mood is violent, challenging, almost heroic in the beginning, and expressed in images of ironworking and military siege, then shifts (though retaining the violence) to the image of erotic ravishment. It is as though he wished to startle, bewilder, or provoke God to some apocalyptic outburst. Herbert, and this is characteristic of his poetry as a whole, is gentle but confident. He acknowledges the necessity of harsh measures, but pleads for softer treatment. There is, furthermore, a profound and subtle theological accuracy in Herbert, which allows him to visualize himself as merely one element in a general pattern of sin and redemption. There is little sense in Donne's *Holy Sonnets* of relationships beyond his with God. We feel with Herbert our kinship with Adam, and, in the quiet **metaphor** which closes the poem ("Fractures well cur'd make us more strong") not only receive the satisfaction of the fulfillment of a pattern of **imagery**, but also the pleasing surprise of such a novel expression of the theological doctrine of the glorified body.

Question: In what ways does Cowley's poetry represent a degeneration of the **metaphysical** style as practiced by Donne and Herbert?

Answer: Cowley's *The Thief*, a random sample of his love lyrics, may serve to illustrate the point. It is not a bad poem, but it lacks Donne's imaginative intensity.

Thou rob'st my Days of bus'ness and delights Of sleep thou rob'st my Nights; Ah, lovely Thief what wilt thou do? What? rob me of Heaven too? Thou even my prayers dost steal from me. And I, with wild Idolatry, Begin, to God, and end them all, to Thee.

Is it a Sin to Love, that it should thus, Like an ill conscience torture us? What e're I do, where e're I go, (None Guiltless e're was haunted so) Still, still, methinks thy face I view And still thy shape does me pursue, As if, not you Me, but I had murthered You.

From Books I strive some remedy to take, But thy Name all the Letters make; What e're 'tis writ, I find That there, Like Points and Comma's everywhere; Me blest for this let no man hold; For I, as Midas did of old, Perish by turning ev'ry thing to Gold.

What do I seek, alas, or why do I Attempt in vain from thee to fly? For making thee my Deity, I gave thee then Ubiquity. My pains resemble Hell in this; The Divine presence there too is, But to torment Men, not to give them bliss.

The first **stanza** is fair enough, though "lovely thief" is a stale image (nothing like Shakespeare's "that sweet thief which sourly robs from me") and it has no relationship what to follows. That is, the poet calls her a lovely thief but nothing in the poem itself justifies the paradox, just as there is nothing in the poem to justify the adjective wild ("wild idolatry"). In the second **stanza**, the line "(None Guiltless e're was haunted so)" is pure filler, adding nothing to the basic conception. The last line of the **stanza** is fresh enough, but it suffers from the awkwardness (exceeding anything in Donne) of the successive monosyllables and the merely confusing collocation of pronouns ("As if, not you Me, but I . . ."). Next, there is nothing inevitable or even logical about the remedy he tries ("Books"), and there is an irritating inexactness about her name making up all the letters in the book, then being seen to resemble a script mangled with excessive punctuation, the whole conceit finally being given the further metaphorical level of Midas' golden touch. The fourth line of the **stanza** ("I gave thee then Ubiquity") is a poor attempt to bring the first three **stanzas** to some kind of focus: 1) she robs him day and night; 2) her shape is "where e're I go"; 3) the letters of her name are "like points and commas everywhere." But what is even worse is the pseudo-theological reference to the "Divine presence" in hell, which evokes even more sacrilegious **connotations** than Donne's "we die and rise the same" (*The Canonization*) precisely because the tone of Cowley's poem is so glib, and Donne's is so impassioned. Furthermore, the basic conceit implied by the title The Thief has been lost sight of altogether. Like many of Cowley's lyrics, it is diffuse, wordy, inexact, and, for the most part, trite, when compared with Donne or Herbert.

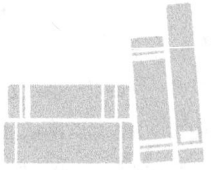

THE METAPHYSICAL POETS

BIBLIOGRAPHY

METAPHYSICAL POETRY (GENERAL)

***Metaphysical** Lyrics and Poems of the Seventeenth Century*, ed. H. J. C. Grierson (Oxford, 1921). Reissued as a Galaxy Book, New York, 1959.

*The **Metaphysical** Poets*, ed. Helen Gardner (Oxford, 1957). Reissued as a Penguin Book, 1961.

DONNE

The Poems of John Donne, ed. H. J. C. Grierson, 2 vols. (London, 1912).

The Divine Poems of John Donne, ed. Helen Gardner (Oxford, 1952).

John Donne: The Anniversaries, ed. Frank Manley (Baltimore, 1963).

The Love Poems of John Donne, ed. Helen Gardner (Oxford, 1965).

The Complete Poetry and Selected Prose of John Donne, ed. Charles M. Coffin (New York; Modern Library, 1952). A convenient and generally reliable one-volume reading text.

CRITICAL STUDIES

Collections of articles and sections of books

A Garland for John Donne, ed. Theodore Spencer (Cambridge, Mass., 1931).

Discussions of John Donne, ed. Frank Kermode (Boston, 1962). A paperback in the D. C. Heath "Discussions of Literature" series.

John Donne: A Collection of Critical Essays, ed. Helen Gardner (Englewood Cliffs, N. J., 1962). A paperback in the Prentice-Hall "Twentieth-Century Views" series.

Seventeenth-Century English Poetry: Modern Essays in Criticism, ed. William Keast (New York: Galaxy Books, 1962).

Books

Pierre Legouis, *Donne the Craftsman* (Paris, 1928).

George Williamson, *The Donne Tradition* (Cambridge, Mass., 1930).

Joan Bennett, *Four **Metaphysical** Poets* (Cambridge, Eng., 1934). Reissued as a Vintage Book, 1960.

Helen C. White, *The **Metaphysical** Poets: A Study in Religious Experience* (New York, 1936).

Charles M. Coffin, *John Donne and the New Philosophy* (New York, 1937).

Robert L. Sharp, *From Donne to Dryden* (Chapel Hill, 1940).

Michael F. Moloney, *John Donne: His Flight From Medievalism* (Urbana, 1944).

Rosemond Tuve, *Elizabethan and **Metaphysical Imagery*** (Chicago, 1947).

J. B. Leishman, *The Monarch of Wit: An Analytical and Comparative Study of the Poetry of John Donne* (London, 1961).

Leonard Unger, *Donne's Poetry and Modern Criticism* (Chicago, 1950).

Doniphan Louthan, *The Poetry of John Donne: A Study in Explication* (New York, 1951).

Clay Hunt, *Donne's Poetry: Essays in Literary Analysis* (New Haven, 1954).

Arnold Stein, *John Donne's Lyrics: The Eloquence of Action* (Minneapolis, 1962).

British Writers and their Work, No. 4, American Edition, ed. J. W. Robinson (Lincoln, Nebraska, 1964). Contains biographical and critical analyses of: Donne (by Frank Kermode); Herbert (by T. S. Eliot); Crashaw, Vaughan, and Traherne (by Margaret Willy).

Articles

H. J. C. Grierson, "Introduction" to his edition (1912).

T. S. Eliot, "The **Metaphysical** Poets," 1921 (included in Kermode, *Discussions*).

Louis I. Brevold, "The Naturalism of Donne," 1923 (included in Kermode, *Discussions*).

William Empson (analyses of a number of lyrics by Donne and the other **metaphysical** poets in his *Seven Types of Ambiguity*, London, 1930). Reissued as a Meridian Book, 1955.

J. E. V. Crofts, "John Donne," 1937 (included in Gardner, *Collection*).

Cleanth Brooks, "The Language of Paradox," (Chapter 1 of *The Well Wrought Urn*, New York, 1947).

Joseph Mazzeo, "Modern Theories of **Metaphysical** Poetry," 1952 (in Kermode, *Discussions*).

Joseph E. Duncan, "The Revival of **Metaphysical** Poetry, 1872 - 1912," 1953 (included in Kermode, *Discussions*).

A. J. Smith, "The Metaphysic of Love," 1958 (included in Kermode, *Discussions*).

INTRODUCTORY WORKS ON THE LITERARY AND CULTURAL BACKGROUND OF THE AGE

Douglas Bush, *English Literature in the Earlier Seventeenth Century*, Oxford History of English Literature, Vol. V, 2nd ed. (Oxford, 1962).

C. S. Lewis, *The Discarded Image: An Introduction to Medieval and Renaissance Literature* (Cambridge, Eng., 1964).

Marjorie Nicolson, *The Breaking of the Circle*, rev. ed. (New York, 1960).

E. M. W. Tillyard, *The Elizabethan World Picture* (London, 1943). Reissued as a Vintage Book.

C. V. Wedgwood, *Seventeenth-Century English Literature* (Oxford, 1950) Reissued as a Galaxy Book.

Basil Willey, *The Seventeenth-Century Background* (London, 1934). Reissued as an Anchor Book. Indispensable.

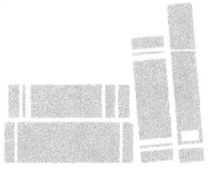

THE METAPHYSICAL POETS

SUBJECT BIBLIOGRAPHY AND GUIDE TO RESEARCH PAPERS

HERBERT

The Works of George Herbert, ed. F. E. Hutchinson (Oxford, 1941).

The Complete Poems of George Herbert, ed. Arthur Waugh (Oxford: World's Classics, 1958).

Marchette Chute, *Two Gentle Men* (New York, 1959).

Joseph H. Summers, *George Herbert: His Religion and Art* (1954).

Rosemond Tuve, *A Reading of George Herbert* (1952).

COWLEY

The English Writings of Abraham Cowley, ed. A. R. Waller, 2 vols. (Cambridge, Eng., 1905).

Robert B. Hinman, *Abraham Cowley's World of Order* (Cambridge, Mass., 1960).

VAUGHAN

The Works of Henry Vaughan, ed. L. C. Martin, 2nd ed. (Oxford, 1957).

Henry Vaughan: Poetry and Selected Prose, ed. L. C. Martin (London: Oxford U.P., 1963).

Ross Garner, *Henry Vaughan: Experience and the Tradition* (Chicago, 1959).

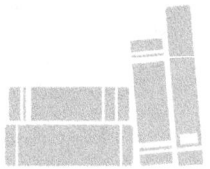

THE METAPHYSICAL POETS

SUGGESTED RESEARCH PAPERS

GENERAL

Project: A history of the term "**metaphysical**" as applied to poetry. What it meant to the various critics who used it, and what **connotations** it developed.

See especially, Sharp, *Donne to Dryden*; Mazzeo, "Modern Theories of **Metaphysical** Poetry."

Project: The relationship between **metaphysical** poetry and the arts. See: Wylie Sypher, *Four Stages of Renaissance Style* (New York, 1956); J. H. Hagstrum, *The Sister Arts: The Tradition of Literary Pictorialism* (Chicago, 1958).

Project: The relationship of **metaphysical** poetry to the world picture of the early seventeenth century. To what extent was "**metaphysical**" imagery a natural expression of the system of analogies and correspondences which were to be the basis of order? See the writings of Marjorie Nicolson and Joseph Mazzeo. In addition, see: Lewis, *The Discarded Image*; E. M. W. Tillyard, *Elizabethan World Picture*.

Project: The **metaphysical** mode in prose. In what respects are the style of prose works like Thomas Browne's *Urn Burial* or Donne's *Devotions* similar to **metaphysical** poetry? See: Willey, *Seventeenth-Century Background*; F. P. Wilson, *Seventeenth-Century Prose* (Berkeley, 1960); George Williamson, *The Senecan Amble* (1951).

DONNE

Project: Donne's religious convictions and changes of sympathy as reflected in his poetry. Did Donne's conversion to Anglicanism modify his medieval Catholic religious outlook, as this can be determined from the poetry? See: Moloney, *Flight From Medievalism*; Gardner (ed.) *The Divine Poems*; Tuve, A *Reading of George Herbert*.

Project: The question of sincerity in Donne's love poetry. Which of the Songs and Sonets have been interpreted as being addressed to Donne's wife? What sort of evidence is there for this? In the case of poems obviously addressed to other women, what can be determined about Donne's actual relationship to them? To what extent do the **conventions** of "complimentary" poetry serve to explain the apparent amatory tone? See: Legouis, *Donne the Craftsman*; Edmund Gosse, *The Life and Letters of John Donne*, 2 vols. (London, 1899); R. C. Bald, *Donne and the Drurys* (1959).

Project: Donne's handling of the **conventions** of the funeral **elegy**. How did the poet use and modify the **themes** and techniques of the **elegy** in such poems as The *First Anniversary* and the Elegie on Prince Henry? See: Ruth Wallerstein, *Studies in Seventeenth-Century Poetic* (Madison, 1950).

Project: The "new science" and Donne's poetry. What awareness does he show of new developments in astronomy, mechanics, and medicine? More important, what is the poetic function of scientific **allusions** in his poetry? (This paper should be severely limited-astronomical **allusions** in the *Songs and Sonets*, for example.) Consult the writings of Marjorie Nicolson. In addition, see: Coffin, *John Donne and the New Philosophy*; D. C. Allen, "John Donne's Knowledge of Renaissance Medicine," *JEGP* (1943).

HERBERT

Projects: George Herbert's debt to Donne. What does Herbert owe to Donne in his style and in his themes? See: Williamson, *The Donne Tradition*.

Projects: The influence of medieval symbolism and theological thought on Herbert. See: Tuve, *A Reading of George Herbert*.

Projects: Herbert and the emblematic tradition. See: Rosemary Freeman, English Emblem Books (1947); Martz, *The Poetry of Meditation*.

COWLEY

Projects: Cowley's interest in the Royal Society and its scientific program. In what ways does the program of the Royal Society manifest itself in: a) Cowley's explicit statements about science and language; b) Cowley's poetic style - especially his choice of metaphors? See: Hinman, *Abraham Cowley's World of Order; Thomas Sprat's History of the Royal Society*, ed. Cope and Jones (St. Louis, 1959).

Projects: The meaning of "wit" for Cowley and his contemporaries. See: W. G. Crane, *Wit and Rhetoric in the Renaissance* (New York, 1937).

VAUGHAN

Projects: Mysticism in Vaughan's poetry. See: Itrat-Husain, *The Mystical Element in the **Metaphysical** Poets of the Seventeenth Century* (1948); E. I. Watkin, *Poets and Mystics* (1953).

www.ingramcontent.com/pod-product-compliance
Lightning Source LLC
LaVergne TN
LVHW011724060526
838200LV00051B/3017